# Aberd Street

## CONTENTS

| | | | |
|---|---|---|---|
| Area of Coverage | 2-3 | Kittybrewster, Old Aberdeen & Tillydrone | 26-27 |
| Central Aberdeen | 4-9 | Craigiebuckler, Hazlehead & Seafield | 28-29 |
| Aberdeen Airport & Dyce | 10-11 | Milltimber & Peterculter | 30-31 |
| Denmore & Middleton Park | 12-13 | Bieldside & Cults | 32-33 |
| Bankhead, Bucksburn & Stoneywood | 14-15 | Braeside, Garthdee & Mannofield | 34-35 |
| Bucksburn, Danestone & Heathryfold | 16-17 | Altens, Balnagask, Nigg, Torry & Tullos | 36-37 |
| Bridge of Don, Hayton & Seaton | 18-19 | Charlestown & Cove Bay | 38-39 |
| Westhill | 20-21 | Portlethen, Portlethen Village & Findon | 40-41 |
| Kingswells, index to Westhill & Kingswells | 22-23 | Muchalls & Newtonhill | 42 |
| Mastrick, Northfield & Sheddocksley | 24-25 | Index to Street Names | 43-52 |

## KEY TO MAP SYMBOLS

|  |  |  |  |
|---|---|---|---|
| A90 | A road dual / single / tunnelled | PO  L | Post Office / library |
| B997 | B road dual / single / tunnelled | P  F | Parking / filling station |
| | Unclassified road | S  H | Supermarket / hospital |
| → | One way / pedestrianised street | +  ✡ | Place of worship / synagogue |
| | Track / path | i  m | Tourist information / museum |
| | Railway / railway tunnel | ⚑  a | Castle / antiquity |
| Aberdeen - Bergen | Ferry route & information | ⚓  ✽ | Historic house / garden |
| ▲  ▼ | Primary / secondary school | ∧  ⊕ | Camping / caravan site |
| △ | Special or independent school |  ✱ | Viewpoint / other interesting feature |
| P  F  A | Police / fire / ambulance station | | Woodland / recreation or cemetery |
| C  L | Coastguard / lifeboat station | | Building / built up area |
| B  ⊟ | Bus / railway station | | Water / sand |

© Copyright Nicolson Maps PU398098 © Crown Copyright reserved.
The maps in this atlas are based upon the Ordnance Survey maps with the permission of Her Majesty's Stationery Office. All rights reserved. Unauthorised reproduction of any part of this atlas, by any means, is a breach of copyright law. Every effort has been made to ensure that the contents of this atlas are correct at the time of printing, the publisher, however, accepts no responsibility for any errors, omissions, or changes in the detail given. The representation of a road, track or footpath is no evidence of a public right of way.

ISBN 1 86097 102 4

## AREA OF COVERAGE

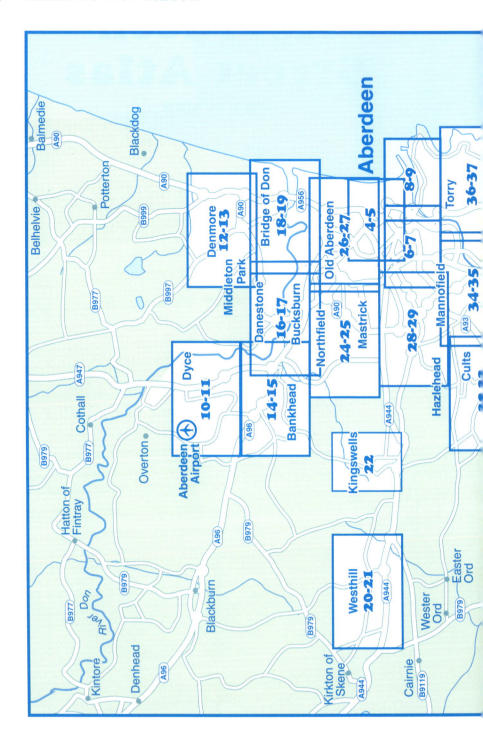

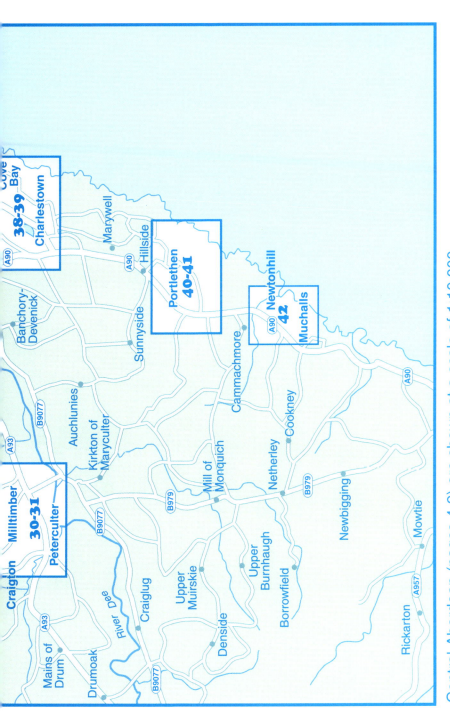

# CENTRAL ABERDEEN

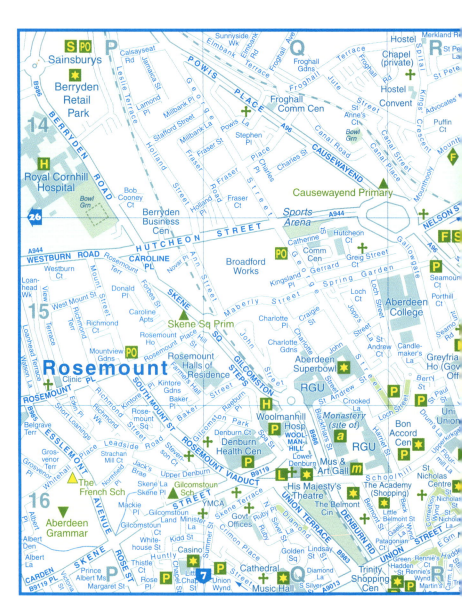

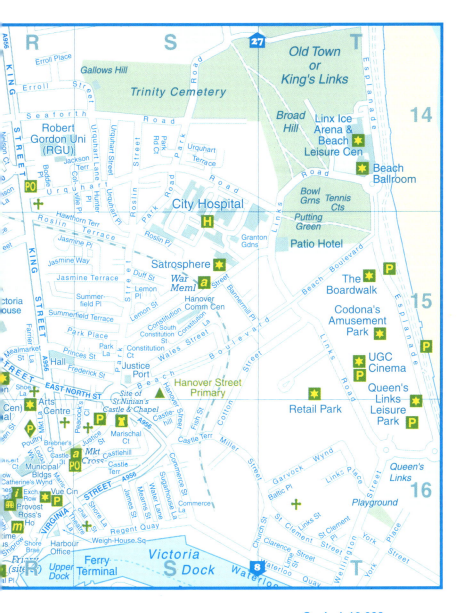

## CENTRAL ABERDEEN

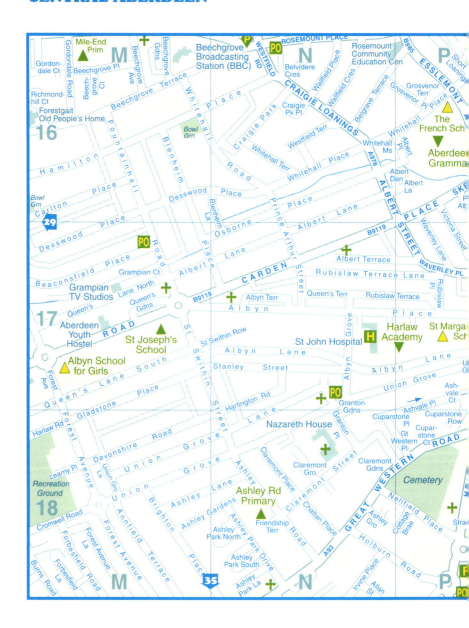

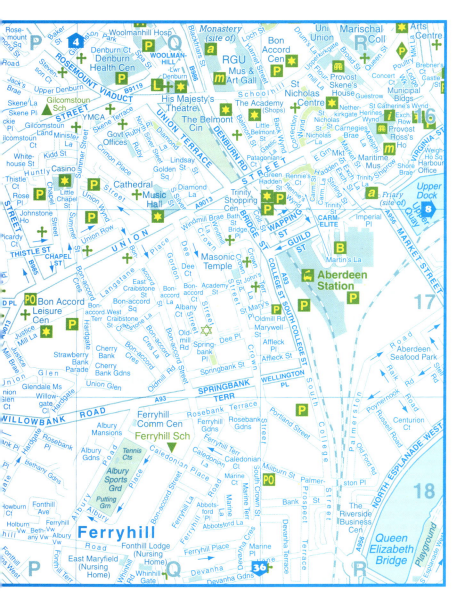

Scale 1:10 000

# CENTRAL ABERDEEN

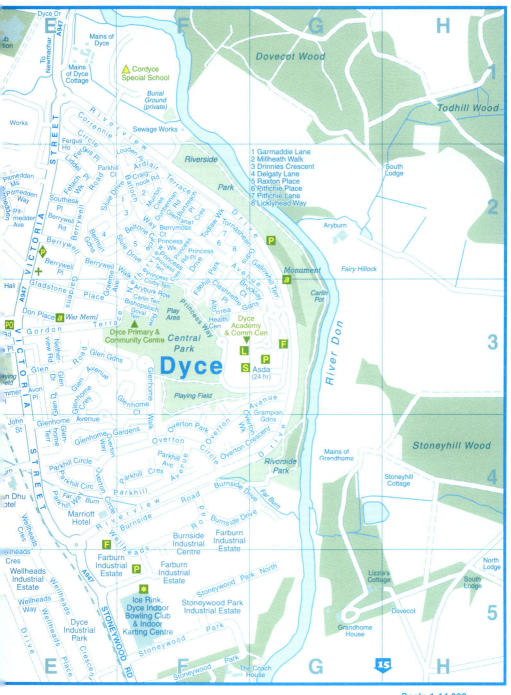

# 12 DENMORE & MIDDLETON PARK

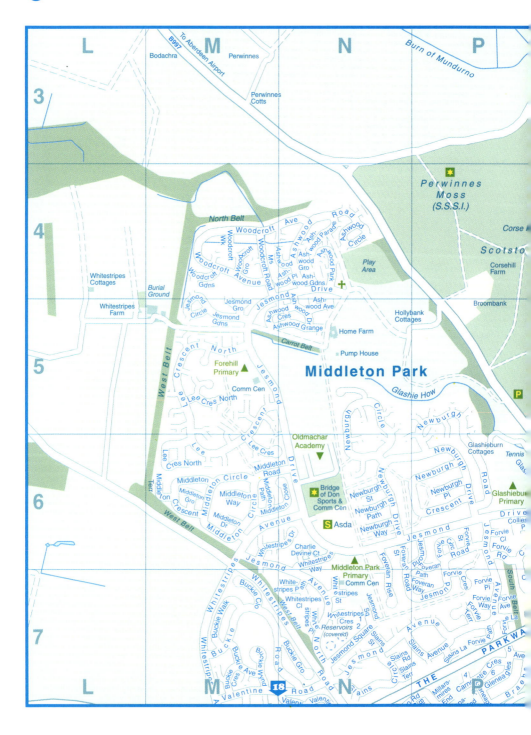

# BANKHEAD, BUCKSBURN & STONEYWOOD

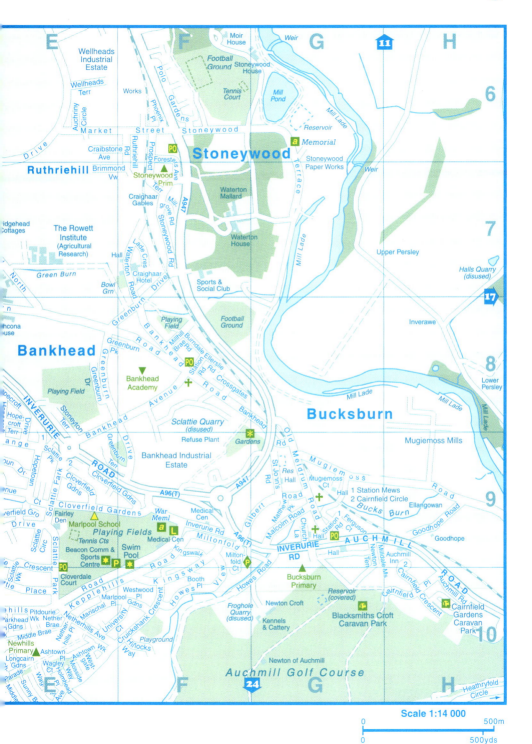

# 16 BUCKSBURN, DANESTONE & HEATHRYFOLD

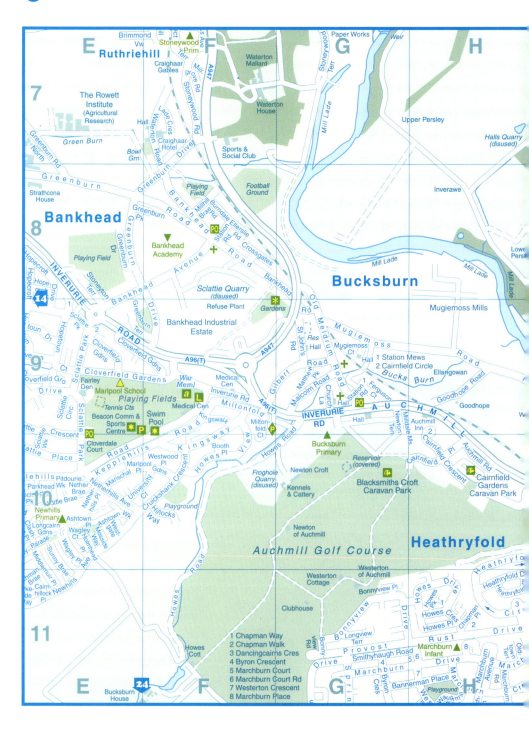

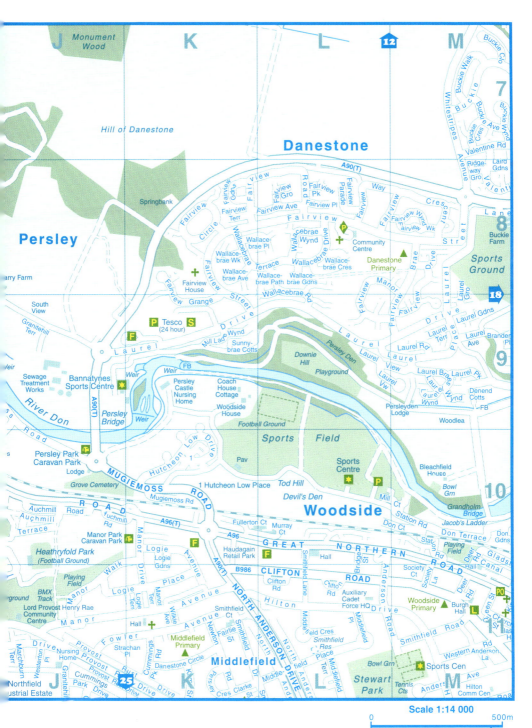

# BRIDGE OF DON, HAYTON & SEATON

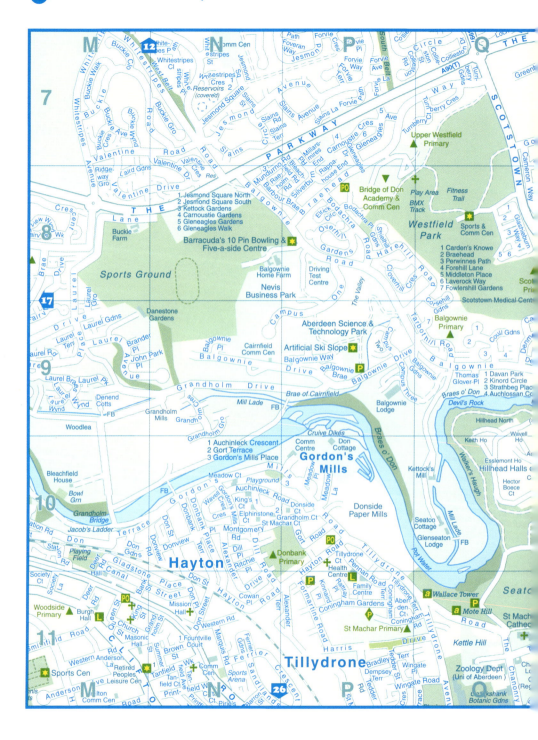

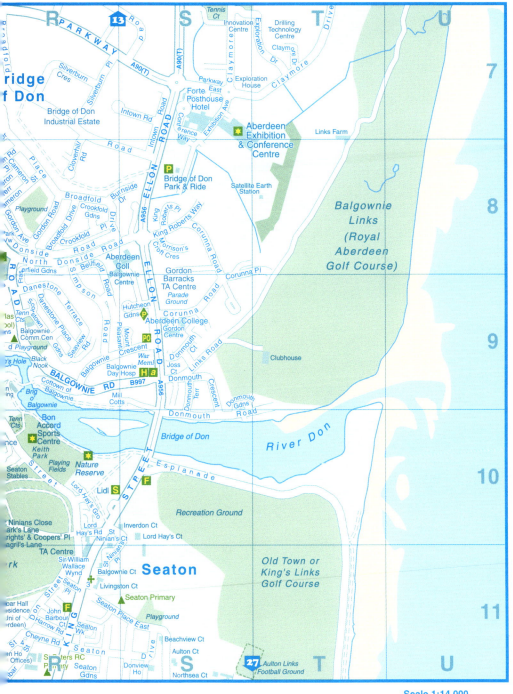

# WESTHILL

Index to street names in Westhill can be found on page 23

# 22 KINGSWELLS

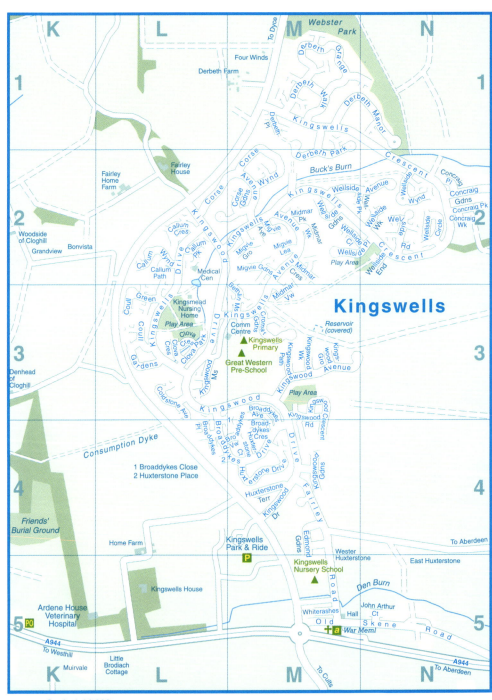

# INDEX TO WESTHILL & KINGSWELLS

**Index to Westhill**

| | | | | | | | |
|---|---|---|---|---|---|---|---|
| Arnhall Cresent | E4 | Dawson Close | B3 | Meadowlands Close | E1 | Broaddykes Place | L3 |
| Arnhall Drive | F4 | Dawson Drive | B3 | Meadowlands Court | D3 | Broaddykes View | L4 |
| Ashdale Close | D3 | Dawson Way | B2 | Meadowlands Crescent | E1 | Callum Crescent | L2 |
| Ashdale Court | E3 | Dawson Wynd | B3 | Meadowlands Drive | D1 | Callum Park | L2 |
| Ashdale Drive | D3, E3 | Dean Gardens | E3 | Meadowlands Park | D1 | Callum Path | L2 |
| Aspen Grove | C4 | Dunecht Gardens | C3 | Meadowlands Place | D1 | Callum Wynd | L2 |
| Barringer Lane | F3 | Dunecht Road | C3 | Meadowlands Way | D1 | Clova Crescent | L3 |
| Beech Road | D4 | Eastside Avenue | E3 | Meikle Gardens | D3 | Clova Park | L3 |
| Beechwood Close | C4 | Eastside Drive | E2 | Morven Circle | D3 | Coldstone Avenue | L3 |
| Beechwood Gardens | C4 | Eastside Green | E2 | Morven Cresent | D3 | Concraig Gardens | N2 |
| Beechwood Place | C4 | Endeavour Drive | E5 | Morven Drive | D3 | Concraig Park | N2 |
| Ben View | A4 | Enterprise Drive | C5 | Morven Gardens | D3 | Concraig Place | N2 |
| Birch Avenue | D4 | Fallow Road | B3 | Mosscroft Avenue | C5 | Concraig Walk | N2 |
| Bishop's Court | F5 | Fare Park Circle | D2 | Moss-side | D4 | Consumption Dyke | K4 |
| Blackhills Court | C4 | Fare Park Crescent | E3 | Mosside Place | D4 | Corse Avenue | L2 |
| Blackhills Place | C3 | Fare Park Drive | D3 | Oak Crescent | D3 | Corse Gardens | M2 |
| Blackhills Way | C4 | Fare Park Gardens | D3 | Oak Drive | D4 | Corse Wynd | M2 |
| Blacklaws Brae | D2 | Fraser Drive | C4 | Old Skene Road | A3, D3 | Coull Gardens | L3 |
| Braecroft Avenue | E3 | Gordon Court | D3 | Old Skene Road | M5 | Coull Green | L3 |
| Braecroft Crescent | E3 | Gordon Gardens (2) | D3 | Parkside | D4 | Cromar Gardens | M3 |
| Braecroft Drive | E3 | Grant Close | D4 | Peregrine Road | B4 | Derbeth Grange | M1 |
| Brimmond Court | D4 | Gulleymoss Gardens | E2 | Rowan Drive | C4 | Derbeth Manor | M1 |
| Brimmond Crescent | D4 | Gullymoss Place | E2 | Shaw Circle | C3 | Derbeth Park | M2 |
| Brimmond Drive | D4 | Gullymoss View | E2 | Souter Circle | E2 | Derbeth Place | M1 |
| Brimmond Lane | D4 | Harvest Hill | B3 | Souter Gardens | E3 | Derbeth Walk | M1 |
| Brimmond Place | D4 | Hay's Way | C3, D3 | Spring Tyne | B3 | Edmond Gardens | M4 |
| Brimmond Walk | D4 | Hazel Drive | D4 | Stanley Court | D4 | Fairley Road | M4 |
| Brimmond Way | D4 | Henderson Drive | C4 | Straik Place | B4 | Huxterstone Court | M4 |
| Broadlands Gardens | B3 | Hillside Crescent | E2 | Straik Road | B4 | Huxterstone Drive | M4 |
| Broadstraik Avenue | B4 | Hillside Gardens | E2 | Strawberryfield Road | A3 | Huxterstone Place (2) | L4 |
| Broadstraik Brae | A4 | Hillside Road | E2, F3 | Trinity Court | E3 | Huxterstone Terrace | M4 |
| Broadstraik Close | A3 | Hillside View | E2 | Wellgrove Crescent | C4 | John Arthur Court | N5 |
| Broadstraik Crescent | A3 | Hilltop Avenue | D2 | Wellgrove Drive | C4 | Kingswells Avenue | M2, M3 |
| Broadstraik Drive | A4 | Hilltop Crescent | D2 | Wellgrove Road | C3 | Kingswells Crescent | M1, M2 |
| Broadstraik Gardens | A3 | Hilltop Drive | D2 | Westdyke Drive | B4 | Kingswells Drive | L3 |
| Broadstraik Grove | A4 | Hilltop Gardens | D2 | Westdyke Avenue | C4, B4 | Kingswood | L3 |
| Broadstraik Road | A4 | Hillview Avenue | E2 | Westdyke Court | B4 | Kingswood Avenue | M3 |
| Broadstraik Place | B4 | Hillview Drive | E2 | Westdyke Gardens | B4 | Kingswood Crescent | M3 |
| Brodiach Court | F3 | Home Lea | B4 | Westdyke Place | B4 | Kingswood Drive | L2, M3 |
| Cairnie View | C2 | Keir Circle | C3 | Westdyke Terrace | B4 | Kingswood Gardens | M4 |
| Cairnton Court | E3 | Kingswells View | D2 | Westdyke Walk | B4 | Kingswood Grove | M3 |
| Carnie Close | B4 | Kinmundy Avenue | E3 | Westdyke Way | B4 | Kingswood Path | M3 |
| Carnie Crescent | B5 | Kinmundy Drive | E3 | Westfield Gardens | D3 | Kingswood Hoad | M3 |
| Carnie Drive | B5 | Kinmundy Gardens | E3 | Westhill Crescent | C3 | Kingswood Road | M4 |
| Carnie Park | B4 | Kinmundy Green | E3 | Westhill Drive | D1, D3, E3 | Kingswood Walk | M3 |
| Carnie Place | B4 | Kirkside Court | E3 | Westhill Grange | C3 | Midmar Crescent | M2 |
| Carnie Way | B5 | Kirkton Avenue | B3 | Westhill Heights | C2 | Midmar Park | M2 |
| Clover Meadow | B3 | Kirkton Gardens | B3 | Westhill Road | E4, F5 | Midmar View | M3 |
| Courtyard, The | C4 | Kirkton Road | B3 | Westwood Crescent | D3 | Midmar Walk | M2 |
| Craigston Gardens | E2 | Larg Drive | B3 | Westwood Drive | D3 | Migvie Avenue | M2 |
| Craigston Place | F2 | Lawsondale Terrace | F3 | Westwood Grove | C3 | Migvie Gardens | M2 |
| Craigston Road | F2 | Lawsondale Avenue | F4 | Westwood Walk (1) | D3 | Migvie Grove | M2 |
| Croft Court | F4 | Lawsondale Drive | F4 | Westwood Way | D3 | Migvie Lea | M2 |
| Crombie Acres | B3 | Lea Rig | B3 | Wrights Walk (3) | E3 | Wellside Avenue | M2 |
| Crombie Circle | B3 | Leddach Gardens | C3 | Wyndford Lane | F3 | Wellside Circle | N2 |
| Crombie Close | B3 | Leddach Place | C3 | | | Wellside Close | M2 |
| Crombie Drive | B3 | Leddach Road | C3 | | | Wellside End | N2 |
| Crombie Place | B3 | Leslie Crescent | C3 | **Index to Kingswells** | | Wellside Gardens | M2 |
| Crombie Road | B3 | Loch View | C2 | | | Wellside Park | M2 |
| Crombie Wynd | B3 | Mains Circle | F3 | Bethlin Mews | M3 | Wellside Place | M2 |
| Cruickshank Court | B4 | Mains Court | F3 | Broaddykes Avenue | M3 | Wellside Road | N2 |
| Dawson Brae | B2 | Mains Gardens | F3 | Broaddykes Close (1) | M4 | Wellside Walk | N2 |
| | | Mains View | F3 | Broaddykes Crescent | M4 | Wellside Wynd | N2 |
| | | Meadowlands Avenue | E1 | Broaddykes Drive | L3 | Whiterashes | M5 |

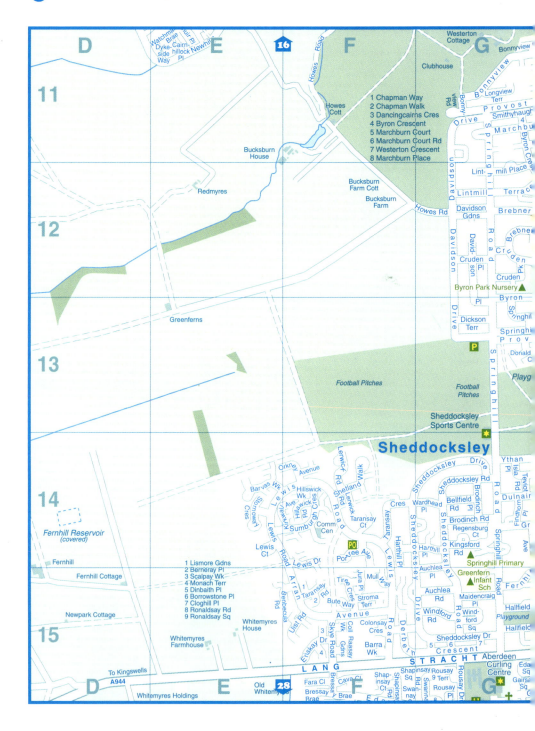

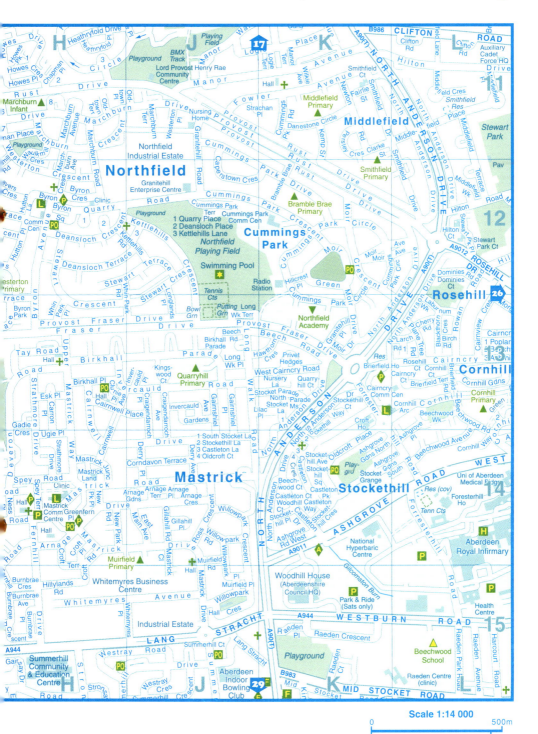

# 26 KITTYBREWSTER, OLD ABERDEEN & TILLYDRONE

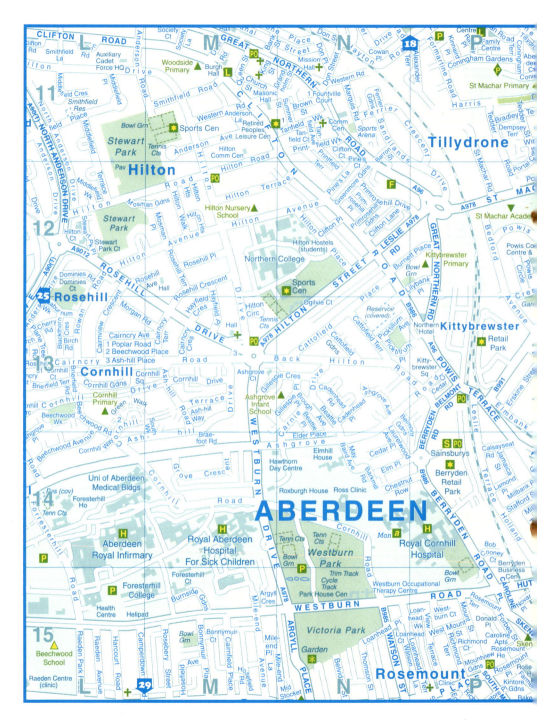

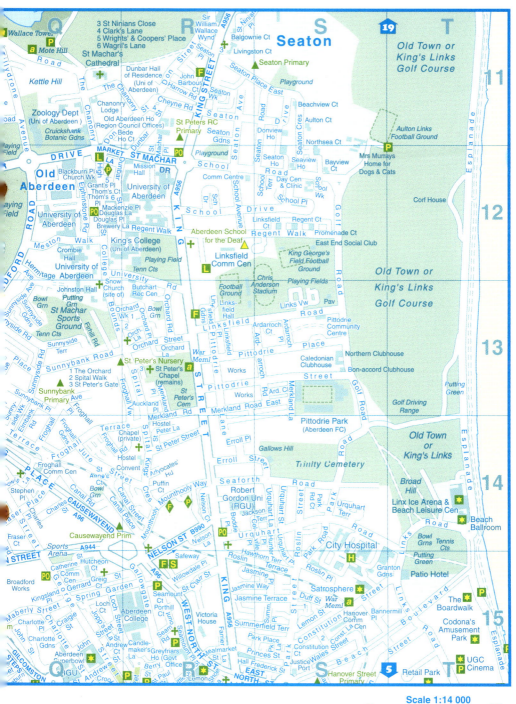

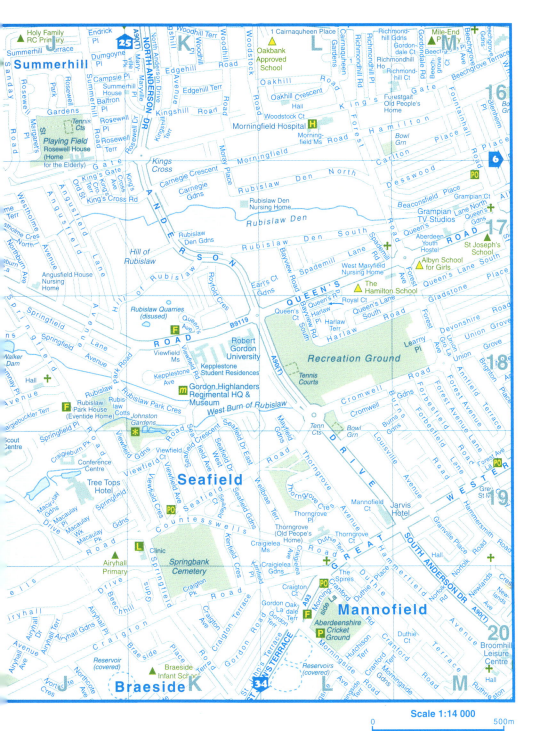

# MILLTIMBER & PETERCULTER

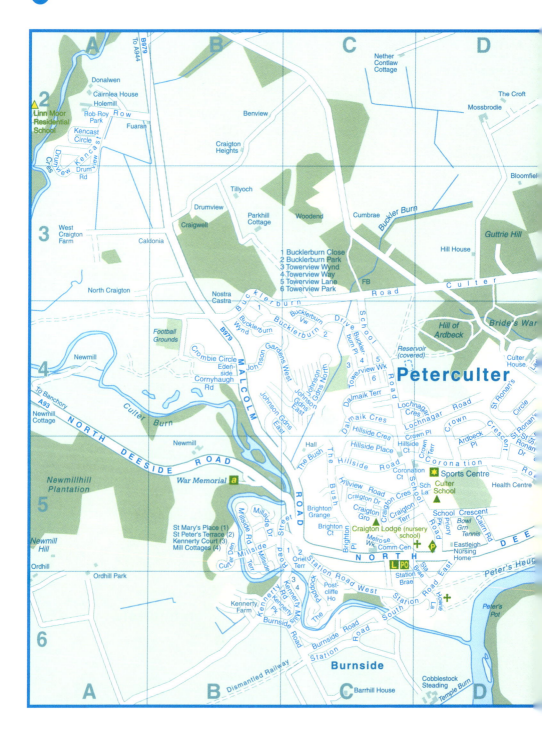

# BIELDSIDE & CULTS

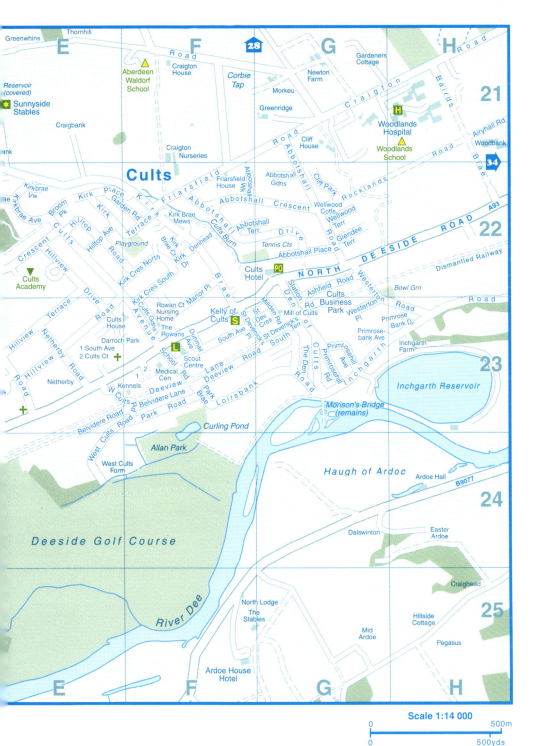

# 34 BRAESIDE, GARTHDEE & MANNOFIELD

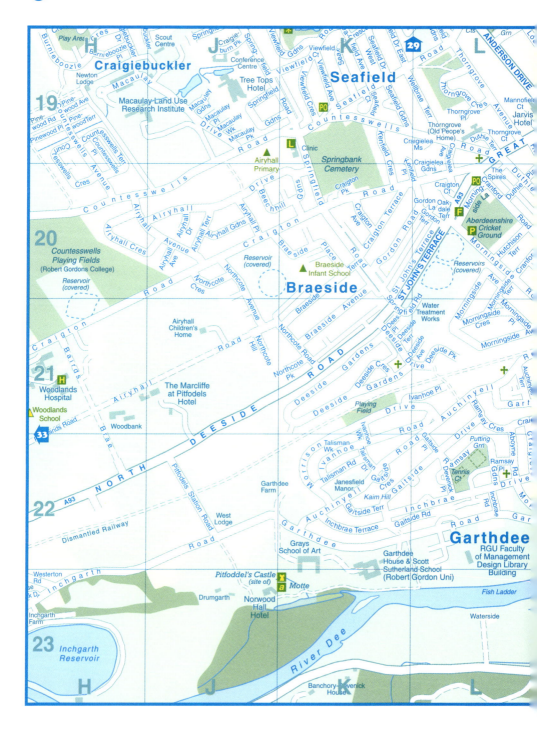

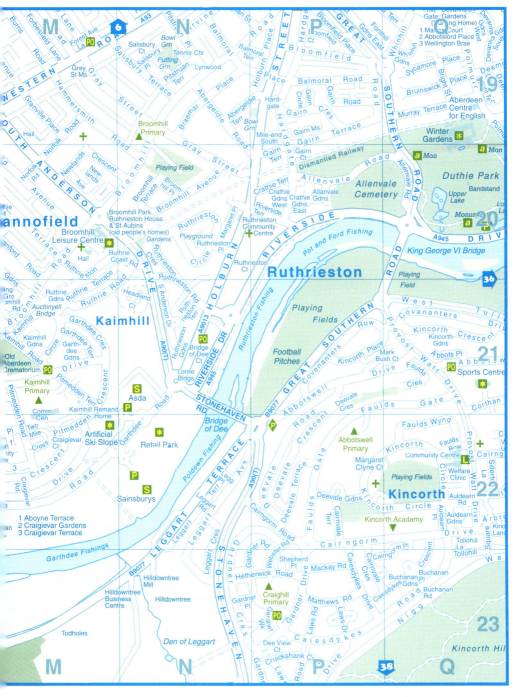

# 36 ALTENS, BALNAGASK, NIGG, TORRY & TULLOS

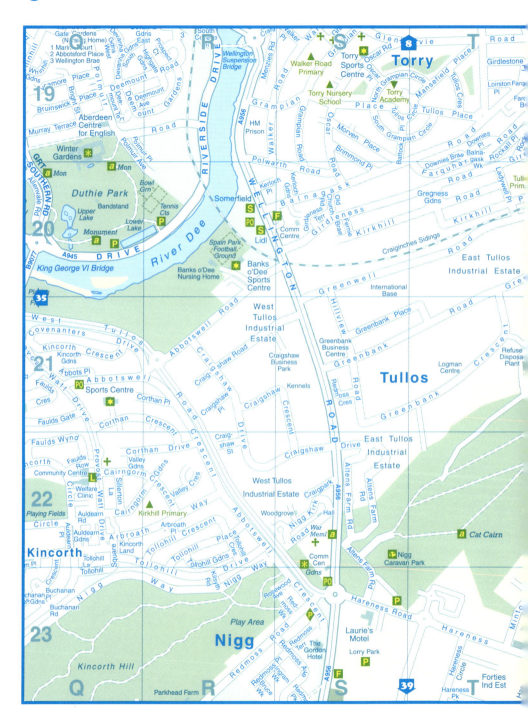

# CHARLESTOWN & COVE BAY

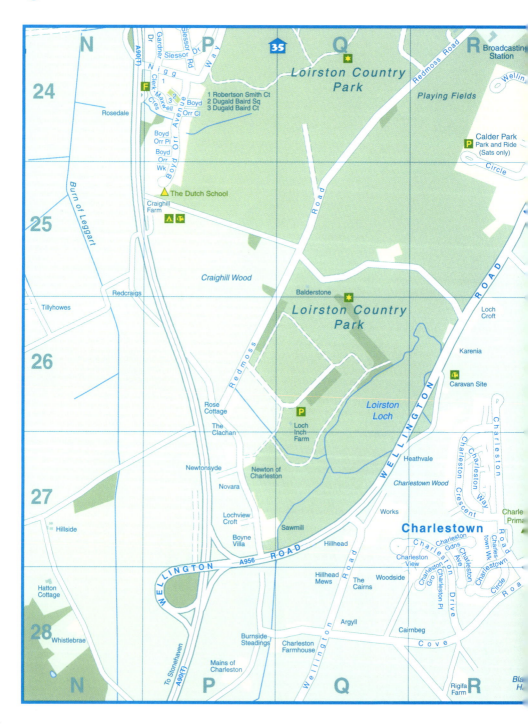

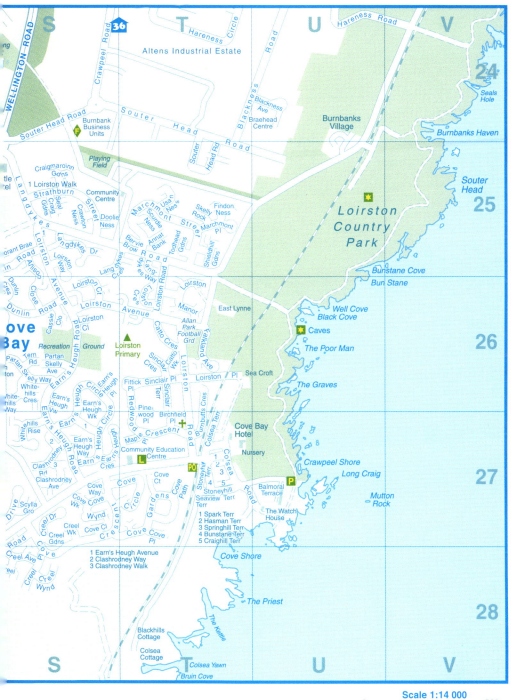

# PORTLETHEN, PORTLETHEN VILLAGE & FINDON

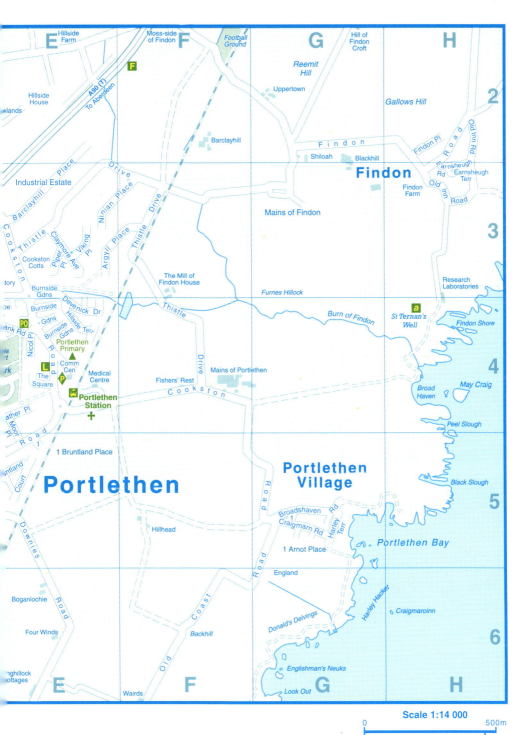

## 42 MUCHALLS & NEWTONHILL

# INDEX TO STREET NAMES

## Index to Portlethen, Newtonhill & Muchalls

|  |  |
|---|---|
| Acorn Place | 40 D6 |
| Alder Drive | 42 C11 |
| Argyll Place | 41 E3 |
| Arnot Place (1) | 41 G5 |
| Ash Court | 40 D5 |
| Ash Grove | 40 D6 |
| Ash Place | 40 D6 |
| Aspen Way | 40 D6 |
| Badentoy Avenue | 40 B2 |
| Badentoy Crescent | 40 A2 |
| Badentoy Place | 40 B3 |
| Badentoy Road | 40 C3 |
| Badentoy Way | 40 A3 |
| Barclayhill Place | 41 E3 |
| Berryhill Place | 42 B11 |
| Berrymuir Place | 40 C6 |
| Berrymuir Road | 40 C6 |
| Berrymuir Wynd (4) | 40 C6 |
| Bettridge Road | 42 C11 |
| Boswell Avenue | 40 C4 |
| Boswell Road | 40 C4 |
| Boswell Walk (2) | 40 C4 |
| Boswell Way (1) | 40 C4 |
| Boswell Wynd | 40 C4 |
| Bourtree Avenue | 40 C6 |
| Bracken Road | 41 E4 |
| Bramble Court | 40 D6 |
| Bramble Place | 40 C6 |
| Bramble Road | 40 D6 |
| Bramble Way | 40 D6 |
| Broadshaven Road | 41 G5 |
| Broomfield Park | 40 C5 |
| Broomfield Road | 40 C5 |
| Bruntland Court | 41 E5 |
| Bruntland Place (1) | 41 E5 |
| Bruntland Road | 40 C6 |
| Burnside Gardens | 41 E4 |
| Cairngrassie Circle | 40 C6 |
| Cairngrassie Drive | 40 C6 |
| Cairnhill Drive | 42 A11 |
| Cairnhill Place | 42 A11 |
| Cairnhill Road | 42 A11 |
| Cairnhill Road | 42 B11 |
| Cairnhill Walk | 42 A11 |
| Cairnhill Way | 42 A11 |
| Cairnwell Drive | 40 D5 |
| Cammach Circle | 40 C6 |
| Chapel Road | 42 C11 |
| Clashfarquhar Crescent | 40 D4 |
| Claymore Avenue | 41 E3 |
| Cliff View | 42 B11 |
| Cookston Cottages | 41 E3 |
| Cookston Road | 41 E3 |
| Cookston Road | 41 F4 |
| Craig Place | 42 C11 |
| Craighead Avenue | 40 D4 |
| Craigmarn Road | 41 G5 |
| Cranhill Brae | 42 C11 |
| Cranhill Place | 42 C10 |
| Crollshilock Place | 42 B11 |
| Crollshilock | 42 B11 |
| Devenick Drive | 41 E4 |
| Downies Road | 41 E5 |
| Drumthwacket Drive (5) | 40 C6 |
| Dunlin Court | 42 C10 |
| Dunnyfell Road | 42 A13 |
| Dunvegan Avenue | 40 D4 |
| Dunvegan Crescent | 40 D4 |
| Dunvegan Place | 40 D4 |
| Earnsheugh Road | 41 H3 |
| Earnsheugh Terrace | 41 H3 |
| Easter Court | 40 D6 |
| Easter Drive | 40 D6 |
| Easter Place | 40 D6 |
| Eastsyde Place (3) | 40 C6 |
| Elsick Place | 42 C11 |
| Fern Drive | 40 D5 |
| Fern Place | 40 D5 |
| Findon Place | 41 H2 |
| Findon Road | 41 G2 |
| Fulmar Court | 42 C10 |
| Glascairn Avenue | 40 D4 |
| Glebe Court | 41 E4 |
| Gorse Circle | 40 C6 |
| Green, The | 40 D5 |
| Greystone Place | 42 C11 |
| Harley Terrace | 41 G5 |
| Headland Court | 42 C11 |
| Heather Place | 41 E4 |
| Heathfield Park | 42 B11 |
| Hillhead Road | 42 C11 |
| Hillside Terrace | 41 E4 |
| Juniper Place | 40 C5 |
| Lethen Walk | 40 C6 |
| Marine Terrace | 42 A13 |
| Marsh Place | 40 D5 |
| Monduff Road | 42 A13 |
| Moor Place | 41 E4 |
| Mosside Crescent | 40 D4 |
| Mosside Drive | 40 D4 |
| Muirend Road | 40 D4 |
| Murray Road | 42 C10 |
| Myrtle Terrace | 40 C5 |
| Nethermains Road | 42 A13 |
| Newton Place | 42 C11 |
| Newton Road | 42 C10 |
| Newtonhill Road | 42 B11 |
| Newtonvale Court | 42 C11 |
| Nicol Park | 40 D4 |
| Nicol Place | 41 E4 |
| Ninian Place | 41 E3 |
| Oak Drive | 40 D6 |
| Old Coast Road | 41 F6 |
| Old Inn Road | 41 H2 |
| Old Inn Road | 41 H3 |
| Old Mill Road | 42 C11 |
| Park Place | 42 B11 |
| Peat Way | 41 E4 |
| Pheppie Road | 42 A13 |
| Piper Place | 41 E3 |
| Plover Court | 42 C10 |
| Puffin Court | 42 C10 |
| Ritchie Place | 42 A13 |
| Rowanbank Road | 40 D4 |
| St Andrews Terrace | 42 B10 |
| St Annes Crescent | 42 B9 |
| St Anne's Wynd | 42 C9 |
| St Crispin's Road | 42 B11 |
| St John's Walk | 42 B9 |
| St Michael's Way | 42 B10 |
| St Michael's Crescent | 42 B10 |
| St Michael's Place | 42 B10 |
| St Michael's Road | 42 B10 |
| St Michael's Walk | 42 B10 |
| St Nathan's Road | 42 B10 |
| St Peter's Road | 42 B10 |
| St Ternan's Road | 42 B11 |
| Sanderling Court | 42 C10 |
| Schoolhill Road | 40 D2 |
| Sedge Place | 40 D5 |
| Skateraw Road | 42 C11 |
| South Headlands Crescent | 42 C11 |
| Square, The | 41 E4 |
| Stranathro Terrace | 42 A13 |
| Tern Court | 42 C10 |
| Thistle Drive | 41 E3 |
| Thistle Drive | 41 F4 |
| Turnstone Court | 42 C10 |
| Viking Place | 41 E3 |
| Villagelands Road | 42 C11 |
| Whinpark Circle | 40 D5 |
| Whiteland Road | 42 C11 |
| Willow Wynd | 40 D5 |
| Windyedge Court | 42 B11 |

## Index to Milltimber & Peterculter

|  |  |
|---|---|
| Ardbeck Place | 30 D5 |
| Avenue The | 31 G3 |
| Bellenden Walk | 31 F4 |
| Binghill Crescent | 31 G3 |
| Binghill Drive | 31 G3 |
| Binghill Hedges | 31 H2 |
| Binghill Park | 31 H3 |
| Binghill Road North | 31 G3 |
| Binghill Road West | 31 G3 |
| Binghill Road | 31 H2 |
| Braehead Terrace | 31 G3 |
| Brighton Court | 30 C5 |
| Brighton Grange | 30 C5 |
| Brighton Place | 30 C5 |
| Bucklerburn Close (1) | 30 C4 |
| Bucklerburn Drive | 30 C4 |
| Bucklerburn Park (2) | 30 C4 |
| Bucklerburn Place | 30 C4 |
| Bucklerburn Road | 30 B4 |
| Bucklerburn View | 30 C4 |
| Bucklerburn Wynd | 30 B4 |
| Burnside Road | 30 C6 |
| Bush, The | 30 C5 |
| Cairn Road | 30 D5 |
| Camphill Estate | 31 F5 |
| Colthill Circle | 31 G3 |
| Colthill Crescent | 31 G2 |
| Colthill Drive | 31 G3 |
| Colthill Road | 31 G3 |
| Contlaw Brae | 31 G3 |
| Contlaw Place | 31 G3 |
| Contlaw Road | 31 F2 |
| Cornyhaugh Road | 30 B4 |
| Coronation Court | 30 C5 |
| Coronation Road | 30 D5 |
| Craigton Crescent | 30 C5 |
| Craigton Drive | 30 C5 |
| Craigton Grove | 30 C5 |
| Craigton Terrace | 30 C5 |
| Crombie Circle | 30 B4 |
| Crown Crescent | 30 D4 |
| Crown Place | 30 C5 |
| Crown Terrace | 30 D5 |
| Culter Den | 30 B5 |
| Culter House Road | 30 D3 |
| Culter House Road | 31 F4 |
| Dalmaik Crescent | 30 C4 |
| Dalmaik Terrace | 30 C4 |
| Drumview Crescent | 30 A2 |
| Drumview Road | 30 A3 |
| Edenside | 30 B4 |
| Hillside Court | 30 C5 |
| Hillside Crescent | 30 C4 |
| Hillside Place | 30 C5 |
| Hillside Road | 30 C5 |
| Hillview Road | 30 C5 |
| Howie Lane | 30 D6 |
| Johnson Gardens East | 30 B4 |
| Johnson Gardens North | 30 C4 |
| Johnson Gardens West | 30 B4 |
| Kencast Circle | 30 A2 |
| Kencast Row | 30 A2 |
| Kennerty Court (3) | 30 C6 |
| Kennerty Mills Road | 30 C6 |
| Kennerty Park | 30 B6 |
| Kennerty Road | 30 B6 |
| Lady's Walk | 30 D4 |
| Lewisvale | 31 E5 |
| Lochnagar Crescent | 30 C4 |
| Lochnagar Road | 30 C4 |
| Malcolm Road | 30 B4 |
| Meadows, The | 31 G2 |
| Melrose Walk | 30 C5 |
| Mill Cottages (4) | 30 C6 |
| Millside Drive | 30 B5 |
| Millside Road | 30 B5 |
| Millside Street | 30 B5 |
| Millside Terrace | e30 B5 |
| Milltimber Brae East | 31 F4 |
| Milltimber Brae | 31 F4 |
| Monearn Gardens | 31 G3 |
| North Deeside Road | 30 A4 |
| North Deeside Road | 30 C5 |
| Oldfold Avenue | 31 G2 |
| Oldfold Crescent | 31 G2 |
| Oldfold Drive | 31 G2 |
| Oldfold Park | 31 G2 |
| Oldfold Place | 31 G2 |
| Oldfold Walk | 31 G2 |
| Oriel Terrace | 30 C5 |
| Paddock, The | 30 C6 |
| Pittengullies Brae | 31 E5 |
| Pittengullies Circle | 31 E5 |
| Postcliffe House | 30 C6 |
| Priory Park | 30 D5 |
| Rob Roy Park | 30 A2 |
| Robertston Place | 31 G4 |
| St Mary's Place (1) | 30 C5 |
| St Peter's Terrace (2) | 30 C5 |
| St Ronan's Circle | 30 D4 |
| St Ronan's Crescent | 30 D5 |
| St Ronan's Drive | 30 D5 |
| St Ronan's Drive | 31 E5 |
| St Ronan's Place | 31 E5 |
| School Crescent | 30 D5 |
| School Lane | 30 D5 |
| School Road | 30 C4 |
| School Road | 30 D5 |
| Station Brae | 30 C6 |
| Station Road East | 30 C6 |
| Station Road East | 31 G4 |
| Station Road South | 30 C6 |
| Station Road West | 30 C5 |
| Station Road | 31 F4 |
| Towerview Lane (5) | 30 C4 |
| Towerview Park (6) | 30 C4 |
| Towerview Walk | 30 C4 |
| Towerview Way (4) | 30 C4 |
| Towerview Wynd (3) | 30 C4 |

## Index to Aberdeen

|  |  |
|---|---|
| Abbey Lane | 8 T18 |
| Abbey Place | 8 T18 |
| Abbey Road | 8 T18 |
| Abbey Square | 37 U19 |
| Abbots Place | 36 Q21 |
| Abbotsford Lane | 7 Q18 |

| | | | | | | | |
|---|---|---|---|---|---|---|---|
| Abbotsford Place | 7 Q18 | Ardarroch Road | 27 S13 | Baillieswells Grove | 32 C23 | Beechwood Road | 26 L13 |
| Abbotshall Crescent | 33 F22 | Ardlair Terrace | 11 F2 | Baillieswells Place | 32 C23 | Beechwood Walk | 25 L13 |
| Abbotshall Drive | 33 F22 | Argyll Close | 10 B5 | Baillieswells Road | 32 C23 | Belgrave Terrace | 6 N16 |
| Abbotshall Gardens | 33 G22 | Argyll Crescent | 26 M15 | Baillieswells Terrace | 32 C23 | Bellfield Road | 24 G14 |
| Abbotshall Place | 33 G22 | Argyll Place | 26 N15 | Baird Avenue | 26 N14 | Bellfield Road | 19 R8 |
| Abbotshall Road | 33 G21 | Argyll Road | 10 B5 | Bairds Brae | 34 H21 | Belmont Gardens | 26 N13 |
| Abbotshall Terrace | 33 F22 | Arnage Crescent | 25 J14 | Baker Place | 4 P15 | Belmont Road | 26 P13 |
| Abbotshall Walk | 33 F22 | Arnage Drive | 25 H14 | Baker Street | 4 P16 | Belmont Street | 7 Q16 |
| Abbotswell Crescent | 36 R22 | Arnage Gardens | 25 J14 | Balfron Place | 29 J16 | Belmuir Gardens | 11 E2 |
| Abbotswell Drive | 35 P21 | Arnage Place | 25 J14 | Balgownie Brae | 18 P9 | Belrorie Circle | 11 F2 |
| Abbotswell Road | 36 R21 | Arnage Terrace | 25 J14 | Balgownie Court | 19 R11 | Belvidere Crescent | 6 N16 |
| Aberden Court | 18 P11 | Arran Avenue | 24 F15 | Balgownie Crescent | 19 R9 | Belvidere Lane | 33 F23 |
| Abergeldie Road | 35 N19 | Aryburk Row | 11 F3 | Balgownie Drive | 18 N9 | Belvidere Road | 33 E23 |
| Abergeldie Terrace | 35 N19 | Ashfield Road | 33 G22 | Balgownie Gardens | 18 Q9 | Belvidere Street | 26 N15 |
| Aboyne Gardens | 35 M21 | Ashgrove Avenue | 26 N13 | Balgownie Place | 18 N9 | Benbecula Road | 24 F15 |
| Aboyne Place | 35 M22 | Ashgrove Court | 26 M13 | Balgownie Road | 18 N8 | Berneray Place (2) | 24 F15 |
| Aboyne Road | 34 L22 | Ashgrove Gardens | 25 K14 | Balgownie Road | 19 R9 | Berry Street | 4 R15 |
| Aboyne Terrace (1) | 35 M22 | North | | Balgownie Way | 18 P9 | Berryden Road | 4 P14 |
| Academy, The (Shopping Centre) | 4 Q16 | Ashgrove Gardens South | 25 K14 | Balloch Way Balmoral Place | 11 F2 35 N19 | Berrymoss Court Berrywell Gardens | 11 F2 11 E2 |
| Academy Street | 7 Q17 | Ashgrove Place | 25 L14 | Balmoral Road | 35 P19 | Berrywell Place | 11 E2 |
| Adam Smith House | 18 Q10 | Ashgrove Road West | 25 K14 | Balmoral Terrace | 35 N19 | Berrywell Road | 11 E2 |
| Adelphi Lane | 5 R16 | Ashgrove Road | 26 N14 | (Mannofield) | | Berrywell Walk | 11 E2 |
| Advocates' Road | 4 R14 | Ash-hill Drive | 26 L14 | Balmoral Terrace | 39 U27 | Bervie Brow | 39 T25 |
| Affleck Place | 7 R17 | Ash-hill Place (3) | 26 M13 | (Cove Bay) | | Bethany Gardens | 7 P18 |
| Affleck Street | 7 R17 | Ash-hill Road | 26 M13 | Balnagask Avenue | 37 U19 | Bethany View | 7 P18 |
| Airyhall Avenue | 28 H20 | Ash-hill Way | 26 M13 | Balnagask Circle | 37 U19 | Bieldside Station | 32 D24 |
| Airyhall Crescent | 28 H20 | Ashley Gardens | 6 M18 | Balnagask Court | 37 U19 | Road | |
| Airyhall Drive | 34 J20 | Ashley Grove | 6 N18 | Balnagask Crescent | 37 U19 | Birch Road | 25 L13 |
| Airyhall Gardens | 34 J20 | Ashley Lane | 6 M18 | Balnagask House | 8 U18 | Birchfield Place | 39 T25 |
| Airyhall Place | 34 J20 | Ashley Park Drive | 6 N18 | Balnagask Road | 36 S20 | Birkhall Parade | 25 H13 |
| Airyhall Road | 34 H21 | Ashley Park Lane | 6 N18 | Balnagask Terrace | 36 U19 | Birkhall Place | 25 H13 |
| Airyhall Terrace | 34 J20 | Ashley Park North | 6 N18 | Balnagask Walk | 36 T19 | Bishopsloch Row | 11 F3 |
| Albany Court | 7 Q17 | Ashley Park South | 6 N18 | Baltic Place | 8 T16 | Blackburn Place | 27 Q12 |
| Albert Den | 6 N16 | Ashley Road | 6 N18 | Bank Street | 18 M11 | Blackfriars Street | 4 Q16 |
| Albert Lane | 6 N17 | Ashtown Place | 15 E10 | Bank Street | 7 R18 | Blackness Avenue | 39 U24 |
| Albert Place | 6 P16 | Ashtown Walk | 15 E10 | Bankhead Avenue | 15 F8 | Blackness Road | 39 U24 |
| Albert Quay | 8 S17 | Ashvale Place | 6 P17 | Bankhead Road | 15 F8 | Black's Lane | 8 S17 |
| Albert Street | 6 N16 | Ashwood Avenue | 12 N5 | Bannerman Place | 24 G11 | Blackthorn Crescent | 25 L13 |
| Albert Terrace | 6 N17 | Ashwood Circle | 12 N4 | Bannermill Place | 5 S15 | Bleachfield Road | 18 P8 |
| Albury Gardens | 7 Q18 | Ashwood Crescent | 12 M5 | Barbour Brae | 18 N8 | Blenheim Lane | 6 N16 |
| Albury Mansions | 7 Q18 | Ashwood Drive | 12 N5 | Barkmill Road | 26 N14 | Blenheim Place | 6 M16 |
| Albury Place | 7 Q18 | Ashwood Gardens | 12 N4 | Barra Walk | 24 F15 | Bloomfield Court | 35 P19 |
| Albury Road | 7 Q18 | Ashwood Grange | 12 N5 | Barron Street | 26 N11 | Bloomfield Place | 35 P19 |
| Albury View | 7 P18 | Ashwood Grove | 12 N4 | Barvas Walk | 24 E14 | Bloomfield Road | 35 P19 |
| Albyn Grove | 6 N17 | Ashwood Mews | 12 N4 | Bath Street | 7 Q17 | Bob Cooney Court | 4 P14 |
| Albyn Lane | 6 N17 | Ashwood Parade | 12 N4 | Battock Place | 36 S19 | Bodachra Place | 18 P8 |
| Albyn Place | 6 N17 | Ashwood Park | 12 N4 | Baxter Court | 9 U18 | Bodachra Road | 18 P8 |
| Albyn Terrace | 6 N17 | Ashwood Place | 12 N4 | Baxter Place | 9 U18 | Boddie Place | 5 R14 |
| Alexander Drive | 18 N10 | Ashwood Road | 12 N4 | Baxter Street | 8 U18 | Bon-accord Court | 7 Q17 |
| Alexander Terrace | 18 P11 | Ashvale Court | 6 P17 | Bayview Court | 27 S12 | Bon-accord Crescent | 7 Q17 |
| Alford Lane | 7 P17 | Auchinleck | 18 N10 | Bayview Road South | 29 L18 | Lane | |
| Alford Place | 7 P17 | Crescent (1) | | Bayview Road | 29 L17 | Bon-accord Crescent | 7 Q17 |
| Allan Street | 6 N18 | Auchinleck Road | 18 N10 | Beach Boulevard | 5 S15 | Bon-accord Lane | 7 Q17 |
| Allenvale Gardens | 35 P20 | Auchinyell Gardens | 35 M21 | Beachview Court | 27 S11 | Bon-accord Shopping | 4 R16 |
| Allenvale Road | 35 P20 | Auchinyell Road | 34 L21 | Beaconhill Road | 32 A25 | Centre | |
| Allison Close | 39 S25 | Auchinyell Terrace | 34 L21 | Beaconsfield Place | 6 M17 | Bon-accord Square | 7 Q17 |
| Altens Farm Road | 36 S22 | Auchlea Place | 24 G15 | Beattie Avenue | 26 N13 | Bon-accord Street | 7 Q17 |
| Altonrea Gardens | 11 F3 | Auchlea Road | 24 G15 | Beattie Place | 26 N13 | Bon-accord Street | 7 Q18 |
| Anderson Avenue | 26 M11 | Auchlossan Court (4) | 18 Q9 | Bede House Court | 27 R11 | Bon-accord Terrace | 7 Q17 |
| Anderson Drive | 29 K17 | Auchmill Road | 16 H9 | Bedford Avenue | 26 P12 | Bonnymuir Court | 26 M15 |
| Anderson Lane | 26 M11 | Auchmill Terrace | 17 J10 | Bedford Place | 27 Q13 | Bonnymuir Place | 26 M15 |
| Anderson Road | 17 L11 | Auchriny Circle | 15 E6 | Bedford Road | 27 Q12 | Bonnyview Drive | 24 G11 |
| Angusfield Avenue | 29 J17 | Auckland Place | 27 R13 | Beech Road | 25 K13 | Bonnyview Place | 24 G11 |
| Angusfield Lane | 29 J17 | Auldearn Gardens | 36 Q22 | Beechgrove Avenue | 6 M16 | Bonnyview Road | 24 G11 |
| Ann Street | 4 P15 | Auldearn Place | 36 Q22 | Beechgrove Court | 6 M16 | Booth Place | 15 F10 |
| Annat Bank | 39 T25 | Auldearn Road | 36 Q22 | Beechgrove Gardens | 6 M16 | Borrowstone Place (6) | 23 G11 |
| Annfield Terrace | 6 M18 | Aulton Court | 27 S11 | Beechgrove Place | 6 M16 | Boyd Orr Avenue | 38 P24 |
| Arbroath Place | 36 R22 | Avon Place | 11 E3 | Beechgrove Terrace | 6 M16 | Boyd Orr Close | 38 P24 |
| Arbroath Way | 36 Q22 | Back Hilton Road | 26 N13 | Beechhill Gardens | 34 J20 | Boyd Orr Place | 38 P24 |
| Ardarroch Close | 27 S13 | Back Wynd | 7 R16 | Beechwood Avenue | 25 L14 | Boyd Orr Walk | 38 P24 |
| Ardarroch Court | 27 S13 | Baillieswells Crescent | 32 C23 | Beechwood Court | 25 K14 | Bradley Terrace | 26 P11 |
| Ardarroch Place | 27 S13 | Baillieswells Drive | 32 C23 | Beechwood Place (2) | 26 L13 | Braefoot Road | 26 M14 |

44

|  |  |  |  |  |  |  |  |
|---|---|---|---|---|---|---|---|
| Braehead (2) | 18 Q8 | Burnside Gardens | 26 M15 | Campus Three | 18 P9 | Chestnut Row | 26 N14 |
| Braehead Way | 18 P8 | Burnside Road | 11 F4 | Campus Two | 18 P9 | Cheyne Road | 27 R11 |
| Braemar Place | 35 N19 | Bute Way | 24 F15 | Canal Place | 4 Q14 | Church Lane | 15 G9 |
| Braeside Avenue | 34 K21 | Bydand Place | 13 R6 | Canal Road | 4 Q14 | Church Street | 18 M11 |
| Braeside Place | 34 K20 | Byron Avenue | 25 H13 | Canal Street | 18 M11 | Church Street | 8 T16 |
| Braeside Terrace | 34 K21 | Byron Crescent (4) | 24 G11 | Canal Street | 4 R14 | Church Walk | 27 Q12 |
| Bramble Brae | 25 K12 | Byron Crescent | 25 H12 | Candlemaker's Lane | 4 R15 | Claremont Gardens | 6 N18 |
| Brander Place | 18 M9 | Byron Park | 25 H13 | Caperstown Crescent | 25 J12 | Claremont Grove | 6 N18 |
| Brebner Crescent | 24 G12 | Byron Square | 25 H12 | Carden Place | 6 N17 | Claremont Place | 6 N18 |
| Brebner Terrace | 24 G12 | Byron Terrace | 24 G12 | Carlin Terrace | 11 F3 | Claremont Street | 6 N18 |
| Brebner's Court | 5 R16 | Cabel's Lane | 8 S18 | Carlton Place | 6 M16 | Clarence Street | 8 T16 |
| Brent Road | 10 C4 | Cadenhead Place | 26 N13 | Carmelite | 7 R17 | Clark's Lane (4) | 27 R11 |
| Bressay Brae | 24 F15 | Cadenhead Road | 26 N13 | Carmelite Lane | 7 R16 | Clarke Street | 25 K11 |
| Brewery Lane | 27 Q12 | Caiesdykes Crescent | 35 Q23 | Carmelite Street | 7 R16 | Clashbog Place | 15 E10 |
| Bridge of Dee Court | 35 N21 | Caiesdykes Drive | 35 P23 | Carnegie Court | 18 Q10 | Clashnettie Place | 11 F3 |
| Bridge Place | 7 Q17 | Caiesdykes Road | 35 P23 | Carnegie Crescent | 29 K17 | Clashrodney Avenue | 39 S27 |
| Bridge Street | 17 L11 | Cairn Crescent | 32 D23 | Carnegie Gardens | 29 K17 | Clashrodney Road | 39 S27 |
| Bridge Street | 7 Q17 | Cairn Gardens | 32 D23 | Carnegies Brae | 7 R16 | Clashrodney Walk (3) | 39 S27 |
| Brierfield House | 25 K13 | Cairn Park | 32 D23 | Carnie Drive | 26 N13 | Clashrodney Way (2) | 39 S27 |
| Brierfield Road | 25 L13 | Cairn Road | 32 D23 | Carnoustie Crescent | 18 P7 | Claymore Avenue | 13 T6 |
| Brierfield Terrace | 25 L13 | Cairn Walk | 32 D23 | Carnoustie Gardens (4) | 18 P7 | Claymore Drive | 13 S7 |
| Bright Street | 36 Q19 | Cairnaquheen Gardens | 29 L16 | Caroline Apartments | 4 P15 | Clerk-Maxwell Crescent | 38 P24 |
| Brighton Place | 6 M18 | | | Caroline Place | 4 P15 | | |
| Brimmond Court | 37 U19 | Cairnaquheen Place (1) | 29 L16 | Carron Place | 25 H13 | Cliff Park | 33 G22 |
| Brimmond Place | 36 S19 | | | Cassie Close | 39 S26 | Clifton Court | 26 N11 |
| Brimmond View | 15 E7 | Cairncry Avenue | 26 L13 | Castle Street | 5 R16 | Clifton Lane | 26 N12 |
| Brimmondside | 14 D10 | Cairncry Court | 25 L13 | Castle Terrace | 5 S16 | Clifton Place | 26 N12 |
| Broad Street | 7 R16 | Cairncry Crescent | 26 M13 | Castlehill | 5 S16 | Clifton Road | 17 L11 |
| Broadfold Drive | 19 R8 | Cairncry Road | 26 L13 | Castleton Court | 25 K14 | Clifton Road | 26 M11 |
| Broadfold Road | 13 R7 | Cairncry Terrace | 26 M13 | Castleton Crescent | 25 K14 | Cloghill Place (7) | 24 G15 |
| Brodinch Place | 24 G14 | Cairnfield Circle (2) | 16 H9 | Castleton Drive | 25 K14 | Cloverdale Court | 15 E10 |
| Brodinch Road | 24 G14 | Cairnfield Crescent | 16 H10 | Castleton Lane (3) | 25 K14 | Cloverfield Court | 14 D9 |
| Brooke Crescent | 13 R6 | Cairnfield Place (Bucksburn) | 16 H10 | Castleton Park | 25 K14 | Cloverfield Gardens (2) | 15 E9 |
| Broom Park | 33 E22 | | | Castleton Way | 25 K14 | Cloverfield Gardens | 15 E9 |
| Broomhill Avenue | 35 N20 | Cairnfield Place (Rosemount) | 26 M15 | Catherine Street | 4 Q15 | Cloverfield Grove | 15 E9 |
| Broomhill Place | 35 N20 | | | Catto Crescent | 39 T26 | Cloverfield Place | 14 D9 |
| Broomhill Road | 35 N20 | Cairnfold Road | 18 Q9 | Catto Walk | 39 T26 | Cloverhill Crescent | 18 P8 |
| Broomhill Terrace | 35 N20 | Cairngorm Crescent | 36 Q22 | Cattofield Gardens | 26 N13 | Cloverhill Road | 19 R8 |
| Brough Place | 26 N13 | Cairngorm Drive | 35 P22 | Cattofield Place | 26 N13 | Clunie Place | 25 H13 |
| Brown Street | 26 N11 | Cairngorm Gardens | 36 Q22 | Cattofield Terrace | 26 N13 | Clyde Street | 8 S17 |
| Bruce House | 28 G17 | Cairngorm Place | 35 Q23 | Causewayend | 4 Q14 | Coach House, The | 11 F5 |
| Bruce Walk | 36 R23 | Cairngorm Road | 35 P22 | Cava Close | 24 F15 | Coll Walk | 24 F15 |
| Brucklay Court | 11 F3 | Cairnhillock Place | 16 E11 | Cedar Court | 26 P13 | College Bounds | 27 Q12 |
| Bruinswick Place | 35 Q19 | Cairnlee Avenue East | 32 D23 | Cedar Place | 26 N14 | College Street | 7 R17 |
| Buchan Road (Dyce) | 10 B3 | Cairnlee Crescent North | 32 D23 | Central Roadway | 8 S17 | Collieston Avenue | 13 Q6 |
| Buchan Road (Balnagask) | 37 U19 | | | Centre Point (2) | 13 R6 | Collieston Circle | 12 P6 |
| | | Cairnlee Crescent South | 32 D23 | Centurion Court | 7 R18 | Collieston Crescent | 13 Q6 |
| Buchanan Gardens | 35 Q23 | | | Chanonry, The | 27 Q11 | Collieston Drive | 13 Q7 |
| Buchanan Place | 35 Q23 | Cairnlee Park | 32 D23 | Chapel Street | 7 P16 | Collieston Path | 12 P6 |
| Buchanan Road | 35 Q23 | Cairnlee Road East | 32 D22 | Chapman Place | 16 H11 | Collieston Place | 12 P7 |
| Buckie Avenue | 12 M7 | Cairnlee Road | 32 C23 | Chapman Walk (2) | 16 H11 | Collieston Road | 12 P7 |
| Buckie Close | 12 M7 | Cairnlee Terrace | 32 C23 | Chapman Way (1) | 16 H11 | Collieston Street | 13 Q7 |
| Buckie Crescent | 12 M7 | Cairnside | 32 D23 | Charles Place | 4 Q14 | Collieston Way | 13 Q6 |
| Buckie Grove | 12 N7 | Cairnvale Crescent | 35 P23 | Charles Street | 4 Q14 | Colonsay Crescent | 24 F15 |
| Buckie Road | 12 M7 | Cairnvale Terrace | 35 P22 | Charleston Avenue | 38 R27 | Colsea Road | 39 T27 |
| Buckie Walk | 12 M7 | Cairnview Crescent | 26 L13 | Charleston Crescent | 38 R27 | Colsea Terrace | 39 T27 |
| Buckie Wynd | 12 M7 | Cairnwell Avenue | 25 H14 | Charleston Drive | 38 R27 | Colville Place | 5 S14 |
| Bunstane Terrace (4) | 39 T27 | Cairnwell Drive | 25 H13 | Charleston Gardens | 38 R27 | Commerce Lane | 5 S16 |
| Bunzeach Place | 11 F2 | Cairnwell Place | 25 H13 | Charleston Grove | 38 R28 | Commerce Street | 5 S16 |
| Burnbank Place | 36 T19 | Caledonian Court | 7 Q18 | Charleston Place | 38 R28 | Commercial Quay | 8 S17 |
| Burnbank Terrace | 37 U19 | Caledonian Lane | 7 Q18 | Charleston Road | 38 R27 | Concert Court | 5 R16 |
| Burnbrae Avenue | 25 H15 | Caledonian Place | 7 Q18 | Charleston View | 38 R27 | Conference Way | 19 S7 |
| Burnbrae Crescent | 25 H15 | Calsayseat Road | 4 P14 | Charleston Walk | 38 R27 | Coningham Gardens | 18 P11 |
| Burnbrae Place | 25 H15 | Cameron Avenue | 18 Q7 | Charleston Way | 38 R27 | Coningham Road | 18 P11 |
| Burnbutts Crescent | 39 T27 | Cameron Drive | 19 R8 | Charlestown Circle | 38 R28 | Coningham Terrace | 18 P11 |
| Burndale Road | 15 F8 | Cameron Place | 19 R8 | Charlie Devine Court | 12 N6 | Constitution Court | 5 S15 |
| Burnett Place | 26 N12 | Cameron Road | 19 R8 | Charlotte Gardens | 4 Q15 | Constitution Lane | 5 S15 |
| Burnieboozle Crescent | 28 H19 | Cameron Street | 19 R8 | Charlotte Place | 4 Q15 | Constitution Street | 5 S15 |
| Burnieboozle Place | 28 H19 | Cameron Terrace | 19 R8 | Charlotte Street | 4 Q15 | Corby Terrace | 11 F3 |
| Burns Gardens | 29 L18 | Cameron Way | 18 Q8 | Chattan Place | 6 N18 | Cordyce View | 10 D3 |
| Burns Road | 6 M18 | Camperdown Road | 26 L15 | Cherry Bank | 7 Q17 | Cormorant Brae | 39 S25 |
| Burnside Drive | 11 F4 | Campsie Place | 29 J16 | Cherry Bank Gardens | 7 Q17 | Corndavon Terrace | 25 J14 |
| Burnside Drive | 19 R8 | Campus One | 18 P9 | Cherry Road | 25 L13 | Cornhill Arcade | 25 L13 |

| | | | | | | | |
|---|---|---|---|---|---|---|---|
| Cornhill Court | 25 L13 | Craignook Road | 11 F2 | Danestone Place | 19 R9 | Dock Street West | 8 T17 |
| Cornhill Drive | 26 L13 | Craigpark | 36 S22 | Danestone Terrace | 19 R9 | Dominies Court | 26 L12 |
| Cornhill Drive | 26 M13 | Craigshaw Crescent | 36 R21 | Darroch Park | 33 E23 | Dominies Road | 26 L12 |
| Cornhill Gardens | 26 L13 | Craigshaw Drive | 36 R21 | Davan Park (1) | 18 Q9 | Don Court | 17 L10 |
| Cornhill Road | 26 M14 | Craigshaw Place | 36 R21 | Davidson Drive | 24 G12 | Don Gardens | 18 M10 |
| Cornhill Road | 26 N14 | Craigshaw Road | 36 R21 | Davidson Gardens | 24 G12 | Don Place (Dyce) | 11 E3 |
| Cornhill Square | 26 L13 | Craigshaw Street | 36 R22 | Davidson House | 28 G17 | Don Place (Hayton) | 18 N11 |
| Cornhill Terrace | 26 L14 | Craigton Avenue | 34 K20 | Davidson Place | 24 G12 | Don Street (Hayton) | 18 N11 |
| Cornhill Way | 26 L14 | Craigton Court | 34 L20 | Deansloch Crescent | 25 H12 | Don Street (Seaton) | 27 Q11 |
| Correction Wynd | 7 R16 | Craigton Park | 34 K20 | Deansloch Place (2) | 25 H12 | Don Street (Seaton) | 19 R11 |
| Corrennie Circle | 11 E1 | Craigton Road | 28 F20 | Deansloch Terrace | 25 H12 | Don Terrace | 18 M10 |
| Corsehill Gardens | 18 Q8 | Craigton Road | 29 J20 | Dee Court | 7 Q17 | Donald Dewar Court | 24 G13 |
| Corthan Crescent | 36 Q21 | Craigton Terrace | 34 K20 | Dee Place | 7 Q17 | Donald Place | 4 P15 |
| Corthan Drive | 36 R22 | Cranford Road | 34 L20 | Dee Street | 7 Q17 | Donbank Place | 18 N10 |
| Corthan Place | 36 R21 | Cranford Terrace | 34 L20 | Dee View Court | 35 P23 | Donbank Terrace | 18 N10 |
| Corunna Place | 19 S9 | Crathie Gardens East | 35 P20 | Deemount Avenue | 36 Q19 | Donmouth Court | 19 S9 |
| Corunna Road | 19 S9 | Crathie Gardens West | 35 P20 | Deemount Gardens | 36 Q19 | Donmouth Crescent | 19 S9 |
| Cothal View | 10 D1 | Crathie Terrace | 35 P20 | Deemount Road | 36 Q19 | Donmouth Gardens | 19 S9 |
| Cottage Brae | 6 P18 | Crawpeel Road | 39 S24 | Deemount Terrace | 36 Q19 | Donmouth Road | 19 S10 |
| Cotton Street | 5 S16 | Crawton Ness | 39 S25 | Deer Road | 18 M10 | Donmouth Terrace | 19 S9 |
| Cottown of Balgownie | 19 R9 | Creel Avenue | 39 S28 | Deeside Avenue | 34 L21 | Donside Court | 18 P10 |
| Coull Gardens | 18 Q9 | Creel Court | 39 S28 | Deeside Crescent | 34 K21 | Donview Place | 18 N10 |
| Countesswells Avenue | 28 H19 | Creel Drive | 39 S27 | Deeside Drive | 34 K21 | Donview Road | 18 N10 |
| | | Creel Gardens | 39 S27 | Deeside Gardens | 34 K21 | Doolie Ness | 39 S25 |
| Countesswells Crescent | 28 H19 | Creel Place | 39 S28 | Deeside Park | 34 L21 | Douglas Lane | 27 Q12 |
| | | Creel Road | 39 S28 | Deeside Place | 34 K21 | Douglas Place | 27 Q12 |
| Countesswells Place | 28 H19 | Creel Walk | 39 S27 | Deeside Terrace (Bieldside) | 32 D25 | Downies Brae | 36 T19 |
| Countesswells Road | 28 F20 | Creel Wynd | 39 S28 | | | Downies Place | 36 T19 |
| Countesswells Road | 29 K19 | Crimon Place | 7 Q16 | Deeside Terrace (Braeside) | 34 K21 | Drinnies Crescent (3) | 11 F2 |
| Countesswells Terrace | 28 H19 | Croft House | 25 K13 | | | Drum's Lane | 4 R16 |
| Cove Circle | 39 T27 | Croft Place | 25 H14 | Deevale Crescent | 35 P22 | Dubford Avenue | 13 Q5 |
| Cove Close | 39 S27 | Croft Road | 25 H15 | Deevale Gardens | 35 P22 | Dubford Crescent | 13 Q5 |
| Cove Court | 39 T27 | Croft Terrace | 25 H14 | Deevale Road | 35 P22 | Dubford Gardens | 13 Q4 |
| Cove Crescent | 39 S27 | Crombie Place | 8 T18 | Deevale Terrace | 35 P22 | Dubford Grove | 13 Q4 |
| Cove Gardens | 39 T27 | Crombie Road | 8 S18 | Deeview Lane | 33 F23 | Dubford Park | 13 Q6 |
| Cove Path | 39 T27 | Cromwell Gardens | 29 L18 | Deeview Road South | 33 F23 | Dubford Place | 13 Q5 |
| Cove Place | 39 T27 | Cromwell Road | 29 L18 | Delgaty Lane (4) | 11 E2 | Dubford Rise | 13 Q4 |
| Cove Road | 38 R28 | Crooked Lane | 4 Q15 | Dempsey Terrace | 26 P11 | Dubford Road | 13 Q6 |
| Cove Walk | 39 S27 | Crookfold Gardens | 19 R8 | Den of Cults | 33 G23 | Dubford Terrace | 13 Q5 |
| Cove Way | 39 S27 | Crookfold Place | 19 R8 | Den, The | 33 G23 | Dubford Walk | 13 Q4 |
| Cove Wynd | 39 S27 | Crossgates | 15 F8 | Denburn Road | 7 Q16 | Duff Street | 5 S15 |
| Covenanters Drive | 36 Q21 | Crown Lane | 7 Q17 | Denend Cottages | 18 M9 | Dugald Baird Court (3) | 38 P24 |
| Covenanters Row | 35 P21 | Crown Street | 7 Q17 | Denhead | 33 F22 | | |
| Cowan Place | 18 N11 | Crown Terrace | 7 Q17 | Denmore Court | 13 R5 | Dugald Baird Square (2) | 38 P24 |
| Craibstone Avenue | 15 E6 | Cruden Crescent | 24 G12 | Denmore Gardens | 18 Q9 | | |
| Craibstone Lane | 7 Q17 | Cruden Park | 24 G12 | Denmore Place | 13 R5 | Dulnain Road | 24 G14 |
| Craig Gardens | 32 D23 | Cruden Place | 24 G12 | Denmore Road | 13 S4 | Dumgoyne Place | 29 J16 |
| Craig Place | 36 R19 | Cruickshank Crescent | 15 F10 | Denseat Court | 28 F16 | Dunbar Street | 27 R12 |
| Craigden | 28 G16 | Cruickshank Crescent | 35 P23 | Denwood | 28 G16 | Dunbennan Road | 11 F2 |
| Craigendarroch Avenue | 25 J13 | Cults Avenue | 33 E22 | Derbeth Crescent | 24 F15 | Dunlin Crescent | 39 S26 |
| | | Cults Court (2) | 33 F23 | Derry Avenue | 25 J14 | Dunlin Road (Cove Bay) | 39 S26 |
| Craigendarroch Place | 25 J13 | Cults Gardens | 33 F23 | Derry Place | 25 J14 | | |
| Craighill Terrace (5) | 39 T27 | Cults House | 33 E23 | Desswood Place | 6 M17 | Dunlin Road (Dyce) | 10 B3 |
| Craigie Loanings | 6 N16 | Cummings Park Circle | 25 K12 | Devanha Crescent | 7 Q18 | Dunmail Avenue | 33 F23 |
| Craigie Park Place | 6 N16 | Cummings Park Crescent | 25 J12 | Devanha Gardens | 7 Q18 | Duthie Court | 35 M20 |
| Craigie Park | 6 N16 | | | Devanha Gardens East | 36 Q19 | Duthie Place | 34 L20 |
| Craigie Street | 4 Q15 | Cummings Park Drive | 25 J11 | | | Duthie Terrace | 34 L20 |
| Craigiebuckler Avenue | 28 H18 | Cummings Park Road | 25 K11 | Devanha Gardens South | 36 Q19 | Dyce Avenue | 10 B4 |
| Craigiebuckler Drive | 28 H19 | Cummings Park Terrace | 25 J12 | | | Dyce Drive | 10 B3 |
| Craigiebuckler Place | 28 H18 | | | Devanha Gardens West | 36 Q19 | Dyce Drive | 14 C7 |
| Craigiebuckler Terrace | 29 J18 | Cuparstone Court | 6 P18 | | | Dyce Drive | 11 E1 |
| Craigieburn Park | 29 J19 | Cuparstone Lane | 6 P18 | Devanha Lane | 7 Q18 | Dykeside Way | 24 E11 |
| Craigielea Avenue | 29 L19 | Cuparstone Place | 6 N18 | Devanha Terrace | 7 R18 | Earl's Court Gardens | 29 K17 |
| Craigielea Gardens | 29 L19 | Cuparstone Row | 6 P18 | Devenick Place | 34 L22 | Earlspark Avenue | 32 C22 |
| Craigielea Mews | 29 L19 | Cypress Avenue | 13 R4 | Deveron Road | 25 H14 | Earlspark Circle | 32 C22 |
| Craigievar Court | 35 M22 | Cypress Grove | 13 R4 | Devonshire Road | 6 M18 | Earlspark Crescent | 32 C22 |
| Craigievar Crescent | 34 L22 | Cypress Walk | 13 Q4 | Diamond Lane | 7 Q16 | Earlspark Drive | 32 C23 |
| Craigievar Gardens (2) | 35 M22 | Dalhebity Court | 32 B22 | Diamond Street | 7 Q16 | Earlspark Gardens | 32 C23 |
| Craigievar Place | 34 L21 | Dalmuinzie Road | 32 B23 | Dickson Terrace | 24 G13 | Earlspark Road | 32 C23 |
| Craigievar Road | 35 M22 | Dancingcairns Crescent (3) | 16 H11 | Dill Place | 18 N10 | Earlspark Way | 32 C22 |
| Craigievar Terrace (3) | 35 M22 | | | Dill Road | 18 N10 | Earlswells Drive | 32 D23 |
| Craigmaroinn Gardens | 39 S25 | Dancingcairns Place | 17 J10 | Dinbaith Place (5) | 24 G15 | Earlswells Place | 32 D23 |
| | | Danestone Circle | 25 K11 | Dock Street East | 8 T17 | Earlswells Road | 32 D23 |

|  |  |  |  |  |  |  |  |
|---|---|---|---|---|---|---|---|
| Earlswells View | 32 D22 | Fairview Terrace | 17 K8 | Forvie Street | 12 P6 | Gillespie Place | 26 N13 |
| Earlswells Walk | 32 D23 | Fairview Walk | 17 M8 | Forvie Terrace | 12 P7 | Girdleness Road | 36 S20 |
| Earn's Heugh Avenue (1) | 39 S27 | Fairview Way | 17 L8 | Forvie Way | 12 P7 | Girdleness Terrace | 36 S20 |
| Earn's Heugh Circle | 39 S27 | Fairview Wynd | 17 M8 | Fountainhall Road | 6 M16 | Girdlestone Place | 36 T19 |
| Earn's Heugh Crescent | 39 S27 | Falkland Avenue | 39 T26 | Fountville Court (1) | 26 N11 | Gladstone Place (Aberdeen) | 6 M17 |
| Earn's Heugh Place | 39 S26 | Fara Close | 24 F15 | Foveran Path | 12 P6 | Gladstone Place (Dyce) | 11 E3 |
| Earn's Heugh Road | 39 S26 | Farburn Terrace | 10 D3 | Foveran Rise | 12 N6 | Gladstone Place (Hayton) | 18 M10 |
| Earn's Heugh View | 39 S26 | Farmers Hall | 4 P15 | Foveran Street | 12 N6 | |  |
| Earn's Heugh Walk | 39 S26 | Farquhar Avenue | 36 T19 | Foveran Way | 12 P7 | |  |
| Earn's Heugh Way | 39 S27 | Farquhar Brae | 36 T19 | Fowler Avenue | 25 J11 | |  |
| East Craibstone Street | 7 Q17 | Farquhar Road | 36 T20 | Fowlershill Gardens (7) | 18 Q9 | Glashieburn Avenue | 12 P6 |
| East Green Market | 7 R16 | Farrier Lane | 5 R15 | Fraser Court | 4 Q14 | Glashieburn Way | 18 Q8 |
| East Main Avenue | 25 J14 | Fassiefern Avenue | 13 R6 | Fraser Place | 4 Q14 | Glen Avenue | 11 E3 |
| East North Street | 5 R15 | Faulds Crescent | 35 Q21 | Fraser Road | 4 P14 | Glen Drive | 11 E3 |
| Eastside Gardens | 14 C8 | Faulds Gate | 35 P22 | Fraser Street | 4 Q14 | Glen Gardens | 11 E3 |
| Eday Court | 28 F16 | Faulds Row | 35 Q22 | Fraserfield Gardens | 19 R8 | Glen Road | 11 E3 |
| Eday Crescent | 24 G15 | Faulds Wynd | 35 Q22 | Frederick Street | 5 S15 | Glenbervie Road | 36 S19 |
| Eday Drive | 24 G15 | Fergus Place | 11 E2 | Friarsfield Road | 33 F22 | Glendale Mews | 7 P17 |
| Eday Gardens | 28 F16 | Ferguson Court | 15 G9 | Friendship Terrace | 6 N18 | Glendee Terrace | 33 G22 |
| Eday Road | 28 H16 | Fernhill Drive | 25 H14 | Froghall Avenue | 4 Q14 | Gleneagles Avenue | 12 P7 |
| Eday Square | 24 G15 | Fernhill Place | 25 H15 | Froghall Gardens | 4 Q14 | Gleneagles Drive | 18 P7 |
| Eday Walk | 28 G16 | Fernhill Road | 24 G15 | Froghall Place | 27 Q13 | Gleneagles Gardens (5) | 18 P7 |
| Eden Place | 4 P15 | Fernie Brae | 36 S20 | Froghall Road | 4 Q14 | Gleneagles Walk (6) | 18 P7 |
| Edgehill Road | 29 K16 | Fernielea Crescent | 28 H16 | Froghall Terrace | 4 Q14 | Glenhome Avenue | 11 E4 |
| Edgehill Terrace | 29 K16 | Fernielea Place | 28 H16 | Froghall View | 27 R13 | Glenhome Court | 11 F3 |
| Elder Place | 26 N14 | Fernielea Road | 28 H16 | Fullerton Court | 17 K10 | Glenhome Crescent | 11 E3 |
| Ellerslie Road | 15 F8 | Ferrier Crescent | 26 N11 | Fyfe House | 18 Q10 | Glenhome Gardens | 11 E4 |
| Ellon Road | 13 S4 | Ferrier Gardens | 26 N11 | Gadie Crescent | 25 H13 | Glenhome Terrace | 11 E4 |
| Ellon Road | 19 S9 | Ferry Place | 8 T17 | Gaelic Lane | 4 R16 | Glenhome Walk | 11 F3 |
| Elm Place | 26 N14 | Ferryhill Gardens | 7 Q18 | Gairn Circle | 35 P19 | Glentanar Crescent | 11 F2 |
| Elmbank Road | 4 Q14 | Ferryhill Lane | 7 Q18 | Gairn Court | 35 P20 | Golden Square | 7 Q16 |
| Elmbank Terrace | 26 P13 | Ferryhill Place | 7 Q18 | Gairn Crescent | 35 P19 | Golf Road (Bieldside) | 32 D24 |
| Elmfield Avenue | 26 P13 | Ferryhill Road | 7 Q18 | Gairn Mews | 35 P19 | Golf Road (Seaton) | 27 S12 |
| Elmfield Place | 26 P13 | Ferryhill Terrace | 7 Q18 | Gairn Road | 35 P19 | Golfview Road | 32 D24 |
| Elmfield Terrace | 27 Q13 | Ferryhill View | 7 P18 | Gairn Terrace | 35 P20 | Goodhope Road | 16 H9 |
| Elmhill House | 26 N14 | Fetach Walk | 11 E2 | Gairnshiel Avenue | 25 J13 | Gordon Avenue | 19 R8 |
| Elphinstone Court | 18 N10 | Fifehill Park | 11 F3 | Gairnshiel Place | 25 J13 | Gordon Lane | 34 L20 |
| Elphinstone Road | 27 Q12 | Findhorn Place | 24 G14 | Gairsay Drive | 25 H15 | Gordon Lennox Crescent | 13 R6 |
| Elrick Circle | 18 P8 | Findon Ness | 39 T25 | Gairsay Road | 24 G15 | Gordon Place | 18 Q7 |
| Endrick Place | 29 J16 | Finnan Brae | 9 U18 | Gairsay Square | 24 G15 | Gordon Road (Braeside) | 34 K20 |
| Eriskay Drive | 24 F15 | Finnan Place | 37 U19 | Gaitside Crescent | 34 K22 | | |
| Erroll Place | 5 R14 | Fintray Road | 28 H18 | Gaitside Drive | 34 K22 | | |
| Erroll Street | 5 R14 | Firhill Road | 27 Q13 | Gaitside Place | 34 L22 | Gordon Road (Br of Don) | 19 R8 |
| Erskine Street | 26 P13 | Fish Street | 5 S16 | Gaitside Road | 34 K22 | | |
| Esk Place | 25 H13 | Fittick Place | 39 T26 | Gaitside Terrace | 34 K22 | Gordon Street | 7 Q17 |
| Esplanade | 19 S10 | Flourmill Lane | 4 R16 | Gallowgate | 4 R15 | Gordon Terrace (Braeside) | 34 L20 |
| Esplanade | 8 U16 | Foinavon Close | 10 D3 | Gallowhill Terrace | 11 G2 | | |
| Esslemont Avenue | 4 P16 | Fonthill Avenue | 7 P18 | Garden Court (3) | 13 R6 | Gordon Terrace (Dyce) | 11 E3 |
| Esslemont House | 18 Q10 | Fonthill Gardens East | 35 P19 | Garden Road | 33 E22 | | |
| Exchange Lane | 7 R16 | Fonthill Gardens West | 7 P18 | Garden's Knowe (1) | 18 Q8 | Gordon's Mills Place (3) | 18 P10 |
| Exchange Row | 5 R16 | Fonthill Road | 7 P18 | Gardner Crescent | 35 N23 | | |
| Exchange Street | 7 R16 | Fonthill Terrace | 7 P18 | Gardner Drive | 38 P23 | Gordondale Court | 6 M16 |
| Exhibition Avenue | 19 S7 | Forbes Street | 4 P15 | Gardner Place | 35 N23 | Gordondale Road | 6 M16 |
| Exploration Drive | 13 T7 | Forbesfield Lane | 6 M18 | Gardner Road | 35 N23 | Gordon's Mills Crescent | 18 N10 |
| Fairies Knowe | 14 D10 | Forbesfield Road | 6 M18 | Gardner Walk | 35 P23 | | |
| Fairlie Street | 25 K11 | Forehill Lane (4) | 18 Q8 | Garmeddie Lane (1) | 11 F2 | Gordon's Mills Road | 18 N10 |
| Fairview Avenue | 17 L8 | Forest Avenue Lane | 6 M18 | Garthdee Crescent | 35 M21 | Gort Road | 18 P10 |
| Fairview Brae | 17 M9 | Forest Avenue | 6 M18 | Garthdee Drive | 34 L21 | Gort Terrace (2) | 18 N10 |
| Fairview Circle | 17 K8 | Forest Road | 29 L16 | Garthdee Gardens | 35 M21 | Goval Terrace | 11 F3 |
| Fairview Crescent | 17 M8 | Foresterhill Court | 26 M15 | Garthdee Road | 34 K22 | Gowanbrae Road | 32 C24 |
| Fairview Drive | 17 M9 | Foresters Avenue | 15 F6 | Garthdee Road | 35 N22 | Graeme Avenue | 11 E3 |
| Fairview Gardens | 17 K8 | Formartine Road | 18 P11 | Garthdee Terrace | 35 M21 | Grampian Court (Aberdeen) | 6 M17 |
| Fairview Grange | 17 K8 | Forresterhill Road | 25 L14 | Garvock Wynd | 8 T16 | | |
| Fairview Grove | 17 L8 | Forrit Brae | 14 D8 | George Street | 4 Q14 | Grampian Court (Balnagask) | 37 U19 |
| Fairview House | 17 K8 | Forties Road | 10 B2 | Gerrard Street | 4 Q15 | | |
| Fairview Manor | 17 L8 | Forvie Avenue | 12 P7 | Gilbert Road | 15 G9 | Grampian Gardens | 11 G3 |
| Fairview Parade | 17 L8 | Forvie Circus | 12 P6 | Gilcomston Park | 4 Q16 | Grampian Lane | 8 S18 |
| Fairview Park | 17 L8 | Forvie Close | 12 P6 | Gilcomston Steps | 4 Q15 | Grampian Place | 36 S19 |
| Fairview Place | 17 L8 | Forvie Crescent | 12 P7 | Gilcomstoun Court | 4 P16 | Grampian Road | 36 S19 |
| Fairview Road | 17 K8 | Forvie Lane | 12 P7 | Gilcomstoun Land | 4 P16 | Grandholm Court | 18 P10 |
| Fairview Road | 17 K8 | Forvie Path | 12 P7 | Gillahill Place | 25 J14 | Grandholm Crescent | 18 N9 |
| Fairview Street | 17 L8 | Forvie Place | 12 P7 | Gillahill Road | 25 J14 | Grandholm Drive | 18 N9 |
| | | Forvie Road | 12 P6 | Gillespie Crescent | 26 M13 | Grandholm Grove | 18 N9 |

**48**

|  |  |  |  |  |  |  |  |
|---|---|---|---|---|---|---|---|
| Grandholm Street | 26 N11 | Hasman Terrace (2) | 39 T27 | Hosefield Road | 26 M15 | Justice Mill Brae | 7 P17 |
| Granitehill Place | 25 K13 | Hawthorn Crescent | 25 K13 | Howburn Court | 7 P18 | Justice Mill Lane | 7 P17 |
| Granitehill Road | 25 J11 | Hawthorn Terrace | 5 R15 | Howburn Place | 7 P18 | Justice Port | 5 S15 |
| Granitehill Terrace | 17 J9 | Hayfield Crescent | 26 M13 | Howe Moss Avenue | 10 A3 | Justice Street | 5 S16 |
| Granton Gardens | 6 N17 | Hayfield Place | 26 M13 | Howe Moss Crescent | 10 A3 | Jute Street | 4 Q14 |
| Granton Place | 6 N18 | Hayton Road | 18 N11 | Howe Moss Drive | 10 A3 | Kaimhill Circle | 35 M21 |
| Grant's Place | 27 Q12 | Hazelhead Avenue | 28 G17 | Howe Moss Place | 10 A3 | Kaimhill Gardens | 35 M21 |
| Granville Place | 35 M19 | Hazelhead Road | 28 G17 | Howe Moss Terrace | 10 A2 | Kaimhill Road | 35 M21 |
| Gray Court | 28 H16 | Hazledene Road | 28 F18 | Howes Crescent | 16 H11 | Keith House | 18 Q10 |
| Gray Street | 35 M19 | Hazlehead Crescent | 28 G17 | Howes Drive | 16 H11 | Kemnay Place | 29 J18 |
| Great Northern Road | 17 L10 | Hazlehead Gardens | 28 G17 | Howes Park | 16 H11 | Kemp Street | 25 K11 |
| Great Northern Road | 26 P12 | Hazlehead Place | 28 G17 | Howes Place | 16 H11 | Kenfield Crescent | 29 K19 |
| Great Southern Road | 35 P21 | Hazlehead Terrace | 28 G17 | Howes Road | 15 F10 | Kenfield Place | 34 K20 |
| Great Western Place | 6 P18 | Headland Court | 35 N21 | Howes Road | 24 G12 | Kepplehills Drive | 15 E9 |
| Great Western Road | 29 L19 | Heathryfold Circle | 16 H11 | Howes View | 15 F10 | Kepplehills Road | 15 E10 |
| Green Hadden Street | 7 R16 | Heathryfold Drive | 16 H11 | Hunter Place | 5 S14 | Kepplestone Avenue | 29 K18 |
| Green Walk | 26 L13 | Heathryfold Place | 16 H11 | Huntly Street | 4 P16 | Kerloch Gardens | 36 S20 |
| Greenbank Crescent | 36 T21 | Hector Boece Court | 18 Q10 | Hutcheon Court | 4 Q15 | Kerloch Place | 36 R20 |
| Greenbank Place | 36 S21 | Herine's Wynd | 5 R16 | Hutcheon Gardens | 19 S9 | Kettlehills Crescent | 25 J12 |
| Greenbank Road | 36 S21 | Hermitage Avenue | 27 Q12 | Hutcheon Low Drive | 17 K10 | Kettlehills Lane (3) | 25 J12 |
| Greenbrae Avenue | 13 R6 | Hetherwick Road | 35 N23 | Hutcheon Low | 17 K10 | Kettlehills Road | 25 J12 |
| Greenbrae Circle | 13 R5 | High Street | 27 Q12 | Place (1) | | Kettock Gardens (3) | 18 N8 |
| Greenbrae Crescent | 13 R5 | Highgate Gardens | 36 R19 | Hutcheon Street | 4 P15 | Kidd Street | 4 P16 |
| Greenbrae Drive | 13 R5 | Hill of Rubislaw | 29 K17 | Hutchison Terrace | 34 L20 | Kildrummy Road | 28 H18 |
| Greenbrae Gardens North | 13 R5 | Hill Street | 4 P15 | Hutton Lane | 25 H12 | Kilsyth Road | 36 R23 |
| | | Hillcrest Place | 25 K12 | Hutton Place | 25 H12 | Kinaldie Crescent | 28 H18 |
| Greenbrae Gardens South | 13 R5 | Hillhead Halls of Residence | 18 Q10 | Hutton Road | 10 C3 | Kincorth Circle | 35 Q22 |
| | | | | Imperial Place | 7 R17 | Kincorth Crescent | 36 Q21 |
| Greenbrae Walk | 13 R5 | Hillhead Road | 32 A23 | Inchbrae Drive | 34 L22 | Kincorth Gardens | 36 Q21 |
| Greenburn Drive | 15 E8 | Hillocks Way | 15 F10 | Inchbrae Road | 34 L22 | Kincorth Land | 36 Q22 |
| Greenburn Park | 15 E8 | Hillswick Road | 24 F14 | Inchbrae Terrace | 34 K22 | Kincorth Place | 35 P21 |
| Greenburn Road North | 14 D7 | Hillswick Walk | 24 F14 | Inchgarth Road | 33 G23 | King Roberts Place | 19 S8 |
| Greenburn Road | 14 D8 | Hilltop Avenue | 33 E22 | Ingram Walk | 36 S23 | King Roberts Way | 19 S8 |
| Greenburn Terrace | 15 E9 | Hilltop Road | 33 E22 | Intown Road | 19 S7 | King Street (Hayton) | 18 M11 |
| Greenfern Avenue | 24 G14 | Hillview Crescent | 32 D22 | Invercauld Gardens | 25 J13 | King Street (Seaton) | 19 R11 |
| Greenfern Place | 25 H14 | Hillview Drive | 33 E22 | Invercauld Place | 25 J13 | King Street | 5 R15 |
| Greenfern Road | 24 G14 | Hillview Road (Cults) | 33 E23 | Invercauld Road | 25 J13 | King's Cross Avenue | 29 J17 |
| Greenhole Place | 13 Q7 | Hillview Road (Tullos) | 36 S21 | Inverdon Court | 19 S10 | King's Cross Road | 29 J17 |
| Greenmore Gardens | 26 N12 | Hillview Terrace | 33 E23 | Inverurie Road | 15 E8 | King's Cross Terrace | 29 J17 |
| Greenwell Place | 37 U20 | Hillylands Road | 25 H15 | Irvine Place | 6 N18 | King's Gate | 28 H17 |
| Greenwell Road | 36 S20 | Hilton Avenue | 26 L12 | Isla Place | 24 G14 | King's Gate | 29 L16 |
| Gregness Gardens | 36 T20 | Hilton Circle | 26 M13 | Ivanhoe Place | 34 L21 | Kingsford Road | 24 G14 |
| Greig Court | 4 Q15 | Hilton Court | 26 L12 | Ivanhoe Road | 34 K22 | Kingshill Avenue | 29 K16 |
| Grey Street Mews | 35 M19 | Hilton Drive | 17 L11 | Ivanhoe Walk | 34 K21 | Kingshill Road | 29 K16 |
| Greyhope Road | 9 V17 | Hilton Drive | 26 M12 | Jack's Brae | 4 P16 | Kingshill Terrace | 29 K16 |
| Groats Road | 28 F17 | Hilton Heights | 26 M12 | Jackson Terrace | 5 R14 | Kingsland Place | 4 Q15 |
| Grosvenor Place | 6 P16 | Hilton Place | 26 N12 | Jamaica Street | 4 P14 | King's Crescent | 4 R14 |
| Grosvenor Terrace | 6 P16 | Hilton Road | 26 L12 | James Street | 5 S16 | Kingswalk | 15 F9 |
| Grove Crescent | 26 M14 | Hilton Street | 26 N13 | Jasmine Place | 5 R15 | Kingsway | 15 F10 |
| Guestrow | 5 R16 | Hilton Terrace | 26 M12 | Jasmine Terrace | 5 R15 | Kingswood Court | 25 J13 |
| Guild Street | 7 R17 | Hilton Walk | 26 M12 | Jasmine Way | 5 R15 | Kinkell Road | 28 H18 |
| Hadden Street | 7 R16 | Holburn Place | 35 P19 | Jesmond Avenue North | 12 N7 | Kinnaird Place | 18 P11 |
| Hallfield Crescent | 24 G15 | Holburn Road | 6 N18 | Jesmond Avenue | 12 N7 | Kinord Circle (2) | 18 Q9 |
| Hallfield Road | 24 G15 | Holburn Street | 6 P18 | Jesmond Circle | 12 M5 | Kintore Gardens | 4 P15 |
| Hamilton Place | 6 M16 | Holburn Street | 35 N21 | Jesmond Drive | 12N4 | Kintore Place | 4 P15 |
| Hammerfield Avenue | 29 M20 | Holburn View | 7 P18 | Jesmond Drive | 12 P6 | Kirk Brae Court | 33 F22 |
| Hammersmith Road | 35 M19 | Holland Place | 4 P14 | Jesmond Gardens | 12 M5 | Kirk Brae Mews | 33 F22 |
| Hanover Street | 5 S15 | Holland Street | 4 P14 | Jesmond Grove | 12 M5 | Kirk Brae | 33 F22 |
| Harcourt Road | 26 L15 | Hollybank Place | 7 P18 | Jesmond Road | 12 P7 | Kirk Crescent North | 33 F22 |
| Hardgate Lane | 35 P19 | Holmhead Place | 15 E10 | Jesmond Square North (1) | 12 N7 | Kirk Crescent South | 33 F22 |
| Hardgate | 7 P19 | Hopecroft Avenue | 15 E8 | | | Kirk Drive | 33 F22 |
| Harehill Road | 18 P8 | Hopecroft Drive | 15 E8 | Jesmond Square South (2) | 12 N7 | Kirk Place | 33 E22 |
| Hareness Circle | 36 T23 | Hopecroft Gardens (1) | 15 E9 | | | Kirk Terrace | 33 E22 |
| Hareness Park | 36 T23 | Hopecroft Terrace | 15 E8 | Jesmond Square | 12 N7 | Kirkbrae Avenue | 33 E22 |
| Hareness Road | 36 T23 | Hopetoun Avenue | 14 D9 | John Barbour Court | 19 R11 | Kirkbrae Drive | 33 E22 |
| Harlaw Place | 29 L18 | Hopetoun Court | 15 E9 | John Park Place | 18 M9 | Kirkbrae View | 33 E22 |
| Harlaw Road | 29 L18 | Hopetoun Crescent | 14 D9 | John Street (Dyce) | 11 E4 | Kirkhill Drive | 10 B2 |
| Harlaw Terrace | 29 L18 | Hopetoun Drive | 15 E9 | John Street (Rosemount) | 4 Q15 | Kirkhill Place | 10 B4 |
| Harriet Street | 4 Q16 | Hopetoun Grange | 14 D8 | | | Kirkhill Place | 36 T20 |
| Harris Drive | 18 P11 | Hopetoun Green | 15 E9 | Johnstone House | 7 P17 | Kirkhill Road | 10 B3 |
| Harrow Road | 27 R11 | Hopetoun Road | 14 D9 | Jopp's Lane | 4 Q15 | Kirkhill Road | 36 S20 |
| Harthill Place | 24 F14 | Hopetoun Terrace | 14 D9 | Joss Court | 19 S9 | Kirkton Avenue | 10 D1 |
| Hartington Road | 6 N17 | Hosefield Avenue | 26 M15 | Jura Place | 24 F15 | Kirkton Drive | 10 C1 |

|  |  |  |  |  |  |  |  |
|---|---|---|---|---|---|---|---|
| Kirkwall Avenue | 24 F14 | Loanhead Place | 26 N15 | Marchburn Drive | 24 G11 | Mile-end Place | 26 M15 |
| Kittybrewster Square | 26 P13 | Loanhead Terrace | 4 P15 | Marchburn Place (8) | 25 H11 | Mile-end South | 35 P19 |
| Laburnum Walk | 25 L13 | Loanhead Walk | 26 P15 | Marchburn Road | 25 H11 | Mill Cottages | 19 R9 |
| Lade Crescent | 15 F7 | Loch Court | 4 Q15 | Marchburn Terrace | 25 J11 | Mill Court | 17 L10 |
| Ladywell Place | 36 T20 | Loch Street | 4 Q15 | Marchmont Place | 39 T25 | Mill Lade Wynd | 17 K9 |
| Laird Gardens | 18 M8 | Lochside Avenue | 13 Q6 | Marchmont Street | 39 T25 | Millarsmires End | 18 P7 |
| Lamond Place | 4 P14 | Lochside Crescent | 13 Q6 | Margaret Clyne Court | 35 P22 | Millbank Lane | 4 P14 |
| Lang Stracht | 25 J15 | Lochside Drive | 13 Q6 | Margaret Place | 35 N20 | Millbank Place | 4 P14 |
| Lang Stracht | 24 F15 | Lochside Place | 13 Q7 | Margaret Street | 7 P16 | Millburn Street | 7 R18 |
| Langdykes Crescent | 39 S25 | Lochside Road | 13 Q6 | Marine Court | 7 Q18 | Milldale Mews | 15 G9 |
| Langdykes Drive | 39 S25 | Lochside Terrace (1) | 13 R6 | Marine Lane | 7 Q18 | Milden Road | 33 G23 |
| Langdykes Road | 39 S25 | Lochview Drive | 13 R6 | Marine Place | 7 Q18 | Miller Street | 5 S16 |
| Langdykes Way | 39 T25 | Lochview Place | 13 Q5 | Marine Terrace | 7 Q18 | Millgrove Road | 15 F7 |
| Langstane Place | 7 Q17 | Lochview Way | 13 R6 | Marischal Court | 5 S16 | Millheath Walk (2) | 11 F2 |
| Larch Road | 25 L13 | Lodge Walk | 5 R16 | Marischal Gardens | 15 E10 | Millhill Brae | 15 F8 |
| Laurel Avenue | 18 M9 | Logie Avenue | 17 K10 | Marischal Street | 5 R16 | Miltonfold | 15 F9 |
| Laurel Braes | 17 M9 | Logie Gardens | 17 K10 | Mark Bush Court | 35 Q21 | Miltonfold Court | 15 F9 |
| Laurel Drive | 17 L9 | Logie Place | 17 J11 | Market Lane | 27 Q12 | Minister Lane | 7 P16 |
| Laurel Gardens | 18 M9 | Logie Terrace | 17 K11 | Market Street | 7 R17 | Minto Avenue | 37 U22 |
| Laurel Grove | 18 M9 | Loirston Place | 39 T26 | (Aberdeen) | | Minto Drive | 37 U23 |
| Laurel Lane | 18 M8 | Loirsbank Road | 33 F23 | Market Street | 14 D7 | Minto Road | 37 U23 |
| Laurel Park | 17 M9 | Loirston Avenue | 39 S25 | (Greenburn) | | Moir Avenue | 25 K12 |
| Laurel Place | 17 M9 | Loirston Close | 39 S26 | Market Street | 15 E6 | Moir Crescent | 25 K12 |
| Laurel Road | 17 M9 | Loirston Court | 39 S26 | (Stoneywood) | | Moir Drive | 25 K13 |
| Laurel Terrace | 17 M9 | Loirston Crescent | 39 T26 | Marlpool Place | 15 E10 | Moir Green | 25 K12 |
| Laurel View | 17 L9 | Loirston Manor | 39 T26 | Marquis Road | 18 N11 | Moir House | 15 F6 |
| Laurel Wynd | 17 M9 | Loirston Place (Torry) | 36 T19 | Martins Lane | 7 R17 | Monach Terrace (4) | 24 F15 |
| Laurelwood Avenue | 26 N14 | Loirston Place | 39 T26 | Maryville Park | 29 K16 | Montgomery Road | 18 N10 |
| Laverock Way (6) | 18 Q8 | (Cove Bay) | | Maryville Place | 29 K16 | Montrose Close | 10 B4 |
| Laws Drive | 35 P23 | Loirston Road | 39 T26 | Marywell Street | 7 R17 | Montrose Drive | 34 L22 |
| Laws Road | 35 P23 | Loirston Way | 39 S25 | Mastick Close | 25 J14 | Montrose Road | 10 B4 |
| Lawson Drive | 10 D2 | Long Walk Place | 25 J13 | Mastrick Drive | 25 H14 | Montrose Way | 10 B4 |
| Leadside Road | 4 P16 | Long Walk Road | 25 J13 | Mastrick Junction | 25 H14 | Monymusk Terrace | 28 H18 |
| Learny Place | 6 M18 | Long Walk Terrace | 25 J13 | Mastrick Land | 25 H14 | Moray Place | 29 K16 |
| Lee Crescent North | 12 M5 | Longcairn Gardens | 15 E10 | Mastrick Road | 25 H14 | Morgan Road | 26 L13 |
| Lee Crescent | 12 M6 | Longlands Place | 25 J13 | Matthew Park | 15 G9 | Morningfield Mews | 29 L16 |
| Leggart Avenue | 35 N22 | Longview Terrace | 24 G11 | Matthews Road | 35 P23 | Morningfield Road | 29 L16 |
| Leggart Crescent | 35 N23 | Lord Hay's Court | 19 S10 | May Baird Avenue | 26 N14 | Morningside Avenue | 34 L21 |
| Leggart Place | 35 N22 | Lord Hay's Road | 19 R10 | Mayfield Gardens | 29 L18 | Morningside Crescent | 34 L21 |
| Leggart Road | 35 N22 | Lord Hay's Grove | 19 R10 | Meadow Court | 18 N10 | Morningside Gardens | 34 L20 |
| Leggart Terrace | 35 N22 | Lorne Buildings | 35 N21 | Meadow Lane | 18 P10 | Morningside Grove | 35 M21 |
| Lemon Place | 5 S15 | Lossie Place | 24 G14 | Meadow Place | 18 P10 | Morningside Lane | 34 L20 |
| Lemon Street | 5 S15 | Louden Place | 11 F2 | Mealmarket Street | 5 R15 | Morningside Place | 34 L21 |
| Lerwick Road | 24 F14 | Louisville Avenue | 29 L19 | Mearns Street | 5 S16 | Morningside Road | 34 L20 |
| Leslie Road | 26 N12 | Lower Denburn | 4 Q16 | Menzies Road | 36 R19 | Morningside Terrace | 34 L21 |
| Leslie Terrace | 4 P14 | Lynwood | 35 N19 | Menzies Road | 8 S18 | Morrison Drive | 34 K22 |
| Lewis Court | 24 E14 | Maberly Street | 4 Q15 | Merkland Lane | 27 S13 | Morrison's Croft | 19 S8 |
| Lewis Drive | 24 F14 | Macaulay Drive | 28 H19 | Merkland Place | 27 R13 | Crescent | |
| Lewis Road | 24 F14 | Macaulay Gardens | 29 J19 | Merkland Road East | 27 R13 | Mortimer Drive | 28 G17 |
| Lickyhead Way (8) | 11 F2 | Macaulay Park | 29 J19 | Merkland Road | 4 R14 | Mortimer Place | 28 G17 |
| Liddel Place | 11 E2 | Macaulay Place | 29 J19 | Meston Walk | 27 Q12 | Morven Court | 37 U19 |
| Lilac Place | 25 J13 | Macaulay Walk | 29 J19 | Mews, The | 10 D1 | Morven Place | 36 S19 |
| Lilybank Place | 26 P12 | Mackay Road | 35 P23 | Mid Stocket Mews | 26 N15 | Mosman Gardens | 26 L12 |
| Lime Street | 8 T16 | MacKenzie Place | 27 Q12 | Mid Stocket Road | 25 K15 | Mosman Place | 26 M12 |
| Lindsay Street | 7 Q16 | Mackie Place | 4 P16 | Midchingle Road | 8 S17 | Mosside Way | 15 E10 |
| Links Place | 8 T16 | Maidencraig Place | 24 G15 | Middle Brae | 15 E10 | Mount Pleasant | 19 S9 |
| Links Road (Br of Don) | 19 S9 | Malcolm Road | 15 G9 | Middlefield Crescent | 17 L11 | Mount Street | 4 P15 |
| Links Road (Footdee) | 5 T15 | Mannofield Court | 29 L19 | Middlefield Place | 17 L11 | Mounthooly Way | 4 R14 |
| Links Street | 8 T16 | Manor Drive | 17 K10 | Middlefield Terrace | 17 L11 | Mounthooly | 4 R14 |
| Links View | 27 S13 | Manor Place | 33 F23 | Middlefield Walk | 26 L12 | Mountview Gardens | 4 P15 |
| Linksfield Court | 27 S12 | Manor Terrace | 17 K11 | Middlemuir Place | 15 E10 | Mugiemoss Court | 15 G9 |
| Linksfield Gardens | 27 R13 | Manor Walk | 17 J11 | Middleton Circle | 12 M6 | Mugiemoss Road | 15 G9 |
| Linksfield Hall | 27 R13 | Manor Avenue | 17 J11 | Middleton Close | 12 M6 | Mugiemoss Road | 17 K10 |
| Linksfield Place | 27 R13 | Manse Road | 32 D23 | Middleton Crescent | 12 M6 | Muirfield Place | 25 J15 |
| Linksfield Road | 27 R13 | Mansefield Place | 36 T19 | Middleton Drive | 12 M6 | Muirfield Road | 25 J14 |
| Lintmill Place | 24 G12 | Mansefield Road | 8 T18 | Middleton Grove | 12 M6 | Muirton Crescent | 11 F2 |
| Lintmill Terrace | 24 G12 | Maple Place | 39 T27 | Middleton Path | 12 M6 | Mull Way | 24 F15 |
| Lismore Gardens (1) | 24 F15 | Marchbank Road | 32 C24 | Middleton Place (5) | 18 Q8 | Mundurno Road | 18 N8 |
| Little Belmont Street | 7 Q16 | Marchburn Avenue | 25 H11 | Middleton Road | 12 M6 | Murray Court | 17 L10 |
| Little Chapel Street | 7 P16 | Marchburn Court (5) | 25 H11 | Middleton Terrace | 12 M6 | Murray Terrace | 35 Q19 |
| Littlejohn Street | 4 R15 | Marchburn Court | 25 H11 | Middleton Way | 12 M6 | Murray's Lane | 8 S18 |
| Livingston Court | 19 R11 | Road (6) | | Mile-end Avenue | 26 M15 | Myrtle Den Road | 32 A24 |
| Loanhead Court | 26 N15 | Marchburn Crescent | 25 H11 | Mile-end Lane | 26 N15 | Myrtle Estate | 32 B25 |

|  |  |
|---|---|
| Nellfield Place | 6 P18 |
| Nelson Court | 5 R14 |
| Nelson Lane | 5 R14 |
| Nelson Street | 4 R14 |
| Ness Place | 25 H14 |
| Nether Brae | 15 E10 |
| Netherby Road | 33 E23 |
| Netherhills Avenue | 15 E10 |
| Netherhills Place | 15 E10 |
| Netherkirkgate | 7 R16 |
| Netherview Avenue | 11 F2 |
| Netherview Road | 11 E3 |
| New Park Place | 25 H14 |
| New Park Road | 25 H14 |
| New Pier Road | 8 U17 |
| Newburgh Circle | 12 N6 |
| Newburgh Crescent | 12 P6 |
| Newburgh Drive | 12 N6 |
| Newburgh Path | 12 N6 |
| Newburgh Place | 12 P6 |
| Newburgh Road | 12 P5 |
| Newburgh Street | 12 N6 |
| Newburgh Way | 12 N6 |
| Newhills Avenue | 14 D10 |
| Newlands Avenue | 35 M20 |
| Newlands Crescent | 35 M20 |
| Newton Road (Dyce) | 10 B3 |
| Newton Road (Middlefield) | 25 K11 |
| Newton Terrace | 15 G9 |
| Nigg Kirk Road | 36 S22 |
| Nigg Way | 36 Q23 |
| Ninian Road | 10 B3 |
| Norfolk Road | 35 M20 |
| North Anderson Drive | 25 K11 |
| North Anderson Drive | 25 K14 |
| North Balnagask Road | 9 U18 |
| North Deeside Road | 32 A25 |
| North Deeside Road | 33 H22 |
| North Donside Road | 19 R8 |
| North Esplanade East | 8 S17 |
| North Esplanade West | 7 R18 |
| North Grampian Circle | 36 S19 |
| North Silver Street | 7 Q16 |
| North Square | 9 U17 |
| North Stocket Lane | 25 K13 |
| Northburn Avenue | 29 J17 |
| Northburn Lane | 29 J17 |
| Northcote Avenue | 34 J20 |
| Northcote Crescent | 34 J20 |
| Northcote Hill | 34 J21 |
| Northcote Park | 34 K21 |
| Northcote Road | 34 K21 |
| Northfield Place | 4 P16 |
| Northsea Court | 27 S11 |
| Novar Place | 4 P15 |
| Nursery Lane | 25 K13 |
| Oakdale Terrace | 34 L20 |
| Oakhill Crescent | 29 L16 |
| Oakhill Road | 29 L16 |
| Ogilvie Court | 26 N13 |
| Old Church Road | 36 S20 |
| Old Ferry Road | 32 C24 |
| Old Ford Road | 7 R18 |
| Old Meldrum Road | 15 G9 |
| Oldcroft Court (4) | 25 K14 |
| Oldcroft Place | 25 K14 |
| Oldmill Road | 7 Q17 |
| Oldtown Place | 17 J11 |
| Oldtown Terrace | 25 H11 |
| Orchard Lane | 27 R13 |
| Orchard Place | 27 R13 |
| Orchard Road | 27 R13 |
| Orchard Street | 27 R13 |
| Orchard, The (1) | 27 R13 |
| Orchard Walk | 27 Q13 |
| Ord Street | 29 J17 |
| Orkney Avenue | 24 F14 |
| Osborne Place | 6 N17 |
| Oscar Road | 36 S19 |
| Oscar Place | 36 S19 |
| Overhill Gardens | 18 P8 |
| Overhills Walk | 14 D10 |
| Overton Avenue | 11 F4 |
| Overton Circle | 11 F4 |
| Overton Crescent | 11 F4 |
| Overton Park | 11 F4 |
| Overton Walk | 11 F4 |
| Overton Way | 11 E4 |
| Oyne Road | 28 H18 |
| Palmerston Place | 7 R18 |
| Palmerston Road | 7 R18 |
| Parade Mews | 25 K13 |
| Park Brae | 33 F23 |
| Park Lane | 5 S15 |
| Park Place | 5 S15 |
| Park Road Court | 5 S14 |
| Park Road (Cults) | 33 F23 |
| Park Road (Seaton) | 5 S14 |
| Park Street | 5 S15 |
| Park View | 19 R8 |
| Parkhead Gardens | 15 E10 |
| Parkhill Avenue | 11 F4 |
| Parkhill Circle | 11 E4 |
| Parkhill Court | 11 E2 |
| Parkhill Crescent | 11 F4 |
| Parkhill Way | 11 E4 |
| Parkway East | 19 S7 |
| Parkway, The | 12 P7 |
| Parkway, The | 13 R7 |
| Partan Skelly Avenue | 39 S26 |
| Partan Skelly Way | 39 S26 |
| Patagonian Court (30) | 7 Q16 |
| Peacock's Close | 5 S16 |
| Pennan Road | 18 P10 |
| Pentland Close | 9 U18 |
| Pentland Crescent | V19 |
| Pentland Place | 37 U19 |
| Pentland Road | 9 U18 |
| Persley Crescent | 25 K11 |
| Perwinnies Path (3) | 18 Q8 |
| Peterseat Drive | 37 U22 |
| Phoenix Place | 15 F6 |
| Picardy Court | 7 P17 |
| Picktillum Avenue | 26 N13 |
| Picktillum Place | 26 N13 |
| Pilot Square | 9 U17 |
| Pinecrest Circle | 32 C22 |
| Pinecrest Drive | 32 B23 |
| Pinecrest Gardens | 32 B22 |
| Pinecrest Walk | 32 B23 |
| Pinewood Avenue | 28 H19 |
| Pinewood Place (Cove Bay) | 39 T26 |
| Pinewood Place (Craigiebuckler) | 28 H19 |
| Pinewood Road | 28 H19 |
| Pinewood Terrace | 28 H19 |
| Pirie's Court | 26 N11 |
| Pirie's Lane | 26 N12 |
| Pitdourie Walk | 15 E10 |
| Pitfichie Lane (7) | 11 F2 |
| Pitfichie Place (6) | 11 F2 |
| Pitfodels Station Road | 34 J22 |
| Pitmedden Avenue | 11 E2 |
| Pitmedden Crescent | 35 M22 |
| Pitmedden Drive | 11 E2 |
| Pitmedden Mews | 11 E2 |
| Pitmedden Road | 10 D1 |
| Pitmedden Road (Dyce) | |
| Pitmedden Road (Garthdee) | 35 M21 |
| Pitmedden Terrace | 35 M21 |
| Pitmedden Way | 11 E2 |
| Pitstruan Place | 35 N19 |
| Pitstruan Terrace | 35 N19 |
| Pittodrie Lane | 27 R13 |
| Pittodrie Place | 27 R13 |
| Pittodrie Street | 27 R13 |
| Plane Tree Road | 25 L13 |
| Polmuir Avenue | 36 Q19 |
| Polmuir Place | 36 Q19 |
| Polmuir Road | 36 Q19 |
| Polo Gardens | 15 F6 |
| Polwarth Road | 36 S20 |
| Poplar Road (1) | 25 L13 |
| Portal Crescent | 26 P12 |
| Portal Terrace | 26 P12 |
| Porthill Court | 4 R15 |
| Portland Street | 7 R18 |
| Portree Avenue | 24 F14 |
| Poultry Market Lane | 5 R16 |
| Powis Circle | 26 P12 |
| Powis Crescent | 26 P12 |
| Powis Lane | 4 Q14 |
| Powis Place | 4 Q14 |
| Powis Terrace | 26 P13 |
| Poynernook Road | 7 R18 |
| Primrosebank Avenue | 33 G23 |
| Primrosebank Drive | 33 H23 |
| Primrosehill Avenue | 33 G23 |
| Primrosehill Drive | 26 N12 |
| Primrosehill Gardens | 26 N12 |
| Primrosehill Place | 26 N12 |
| Primrosehill Road | 33 G23 |
| Prince Albert Mews | 6 P16 |
| Prince Arthur Street | 6 N17 |
| Princes Street | 5 R15 |
| Princess Crescent | 11 F2 |
| Princess Drive | 11 F2 |
| Princess Place | 11 F2 |
| Princess Road | 11 F2 |
| Princess Terrace | 11 F2 |
| Princess Walk | 11 F2 |
| Princess Way | 11 F3 |
| Printfield Terrace | 26 N11 |
| Printfield Walk | 26 N11 |
| Privet Hedges | 25 K13 |
| Promenade Court | 27 S12 |
| Prospect Court | 36 R19 |
| Prospect House | 8 U17 |
| Prospect Terrace (Stoneywood) | 15 F6 |
| Prospect Terrace (Ferryhill) | 7 R18 |
| Prospectthill Road | 32 C24 |
| Provost Fraser Drive | 25 H13 |
| Provost Graham Avenue | 28 G17 |
| Provost Hogg Court | 8 U18 |
| Provost Mitchell Circle | 13 R4 |
| Provost Rust Drive | 25 J11 |
| Provost Watt Drive | 35 Q21 |
| Puffin Court | 4 R14 |
| Quarry Court | 33 E23 |
| Quarry Place (1) | 25 H12 |
| Quarry Road (Bieldside) | 32 D23 |
| Quarry Road (Northfield) | 25 H12 |
| Quarryhill Court | 25 K13 |
| Queen Street (Aberdeen) | 5 R16 |
| Queen Street (Woodside) | 18 M11 |
| Queen's Court | 29 L18 |
| Queen's Avenue | 29 K18 |
| Queens Den | 28 F16 |
| Queen's Gardens | 6 M17 |
| Queen's Lane North | 6 M17 |
| Queen's Lane South | 6 M17 |
| Queen's Road | 28 H17 |
| Queen's Terrace | 6 N17 |
| Raasay Gardens | 24 F15 |
| Raeburn Place | 4 Q16 |
| Raeden Avenue | 26 L15 |
| Raeden Court | 25 K15 |
| Raeden Crescent | 25 K15 |
| Raeden Park Road | 26 L15 |
| Raeden Place | 25 K15 |
| Raeholm Road | 18 N8 |
| Raik Road | 7 R17 |
| Ramsay Crescent | 34 L21 |
| Ramsay Gardens | 34 L22 |
| Ramsay Place | 34 L22 |
| Rappahouse End | 18 P8 |
| Rattray Place | 18 P11 |
| Raxton Place (5) | 11 F2 |
| Redmoss Avenue | 36 S23 |
| Redmoss Crescent | 36 S21 |
| Redmoss Park | 36 S23 |
| Redmoss Place | 36 R23 |
| Redmoss Road | 38 P26 |
| Redmoss Terrace | 36 S23 |
| Redmoss Walk | 36 S23 |
| Redwood Crescent | 39 T27 |
| Regensburgh Court | 24 G14 |
| Regent Central | 8 S17 |
| Regent Court | 27 S12 |
| Regent Quay | 5 S16 |
| Regent Road | 8 S17 |
| Regent Walk | 27 R12 |
| Regent Walk | 27 S12 |
| Rennie's Court | 7 R16 |
| Rennie's Wynd | 7 R16 |
| Richmond Court | 4 P15 |
| Richmond Street | 4 P15 |
| Richmond Terrace | 4 P15 |
| Richmond Walk | 4 P16 |
| Richmondhill Court | 6 M16 |
| Richmondhill Gardens | 29 M15 |
| Richmondhill House | 29 L16 |
| Richmondhill Place | 29 L16 |
| Richmondhill Road | 29 L16 |
| Ridgeway Grove | 18 M8 |
| Ritchie Place | 18 N10 |
| Riverside Drive | 35 N21 |
| Riverside Drive | 36 R19 |
| Riverside Terrace | 35 P20 |
| Riverview Drive | 11 E1 |
| Riverview Drive | 11 E4 |
| Robertson Smith Court (1) | 38 P24 |
| Rockall Place | 36 T19 |
| Rockall Road | 36 T19 |
| Rocklands Road | 33 G22 |
| Ronaldsay Road (8) | 24 G15 |
| Ronaldsay Square (9) | 24 G15 |
| Rose House | 28 G17 |
| Rose Place | 7 P16 |
| Rose Street | 7 P16 |

| | | | | | | | |
|---|---|---|---|---|---|---|---|
| Rosebank Gardens | 7 Q18 | St John's Terrace | 34 K20 | Seaview Crescent | 13 R4 | South Walk | 26 M13 |
| Rosebank Place | 7 P18 | St Machar Court | 18 N10 | Seaview Drive | 13 R5 | South Court | 36 R19 |
| Rosebank Terrace | 7 Q18 | St Machar Drive | 26 P12 | Seaview Place | 13 R4 | Southesk Place | 11 E2 |
| Rosebery Street | 26 M15 | St Machar Drive | 27 R12 | Seaview Road | 19 R9 | Spa Street | 4 Q16 |
| Rosehill Avenue | 26 L12 | St Machar Place | 27 R12 | Seaview Terrace | 39 T27 | Spademill Lane | 29 L17 |
| Rosehill Court | 25 L13 | St Machar Road | 26 P12 | Shapinsay Court | 24 F15 | Spademill Road | 29 L17 |
| Rosehill Crescent | 26 M12 | St Margaret's Place | 29 J16 | Shapinsay Road | 24 F15 | Spark Terrace (1) | 39 T27 |
| Rosehill Drive | 26 L12 | St Mary's Place | 7 Q17 | Shapinsay Square | 24 F15 | Spey Road | 25 H14 |
| Rosehill Place | 26 M12 | St Nicholas Shopping | 4 R16 | Sheddocksley Drive | 24 G14 | Spey Terrace | 25 H14 |
| Rosehill Terrace | 26 M12 | Centre | | Sheddocksley Road | 24 G14 | Spires, The | 34 L20 |
| Rosemount House | 4 P15 | St Nicholas Lane | 7 R16 | Shepherd Place | 35 P23 | Spital Walk (2) | 27 R13 |
| Rosemount Place | 4 P15 | St Nicholas Street | 7 R16 | Shetland Walk | 24 F14 | Spital | 27 R13 |
| Rosemount Square | 4 P15 | St Ninian's Close (3) | 19 R11 | Shieldhill Gardens | 39 T25 | Spring Garden | 4 Q15 |
| Rosemount Terrace | 4 P15 | St Ninian's Court | 19 R10 | Shielhill Gardens | 18 P8 | Springbank Place | 7 Q17 |
| Rosemount Viaduct | 4 Q16 | St Ninian's Place | 19 R11 | Shiprow | 7 R16 | Springbank Street | 7 Q17 |
| Rosewell Drive | 29 K16 | St Paul Street | 4 R15 | Shoe Lane | 5 R15 | Springbank Terrace | 7 Q17 |
| Rosewell Gardens | 29 J16 | St Peter Lane | 4 R14 | Shore Brae | 5 R16 | Springdale Court | 32 C23 |
| Rosewell Park | 29 J16 | St Peter Street | 4 R14 | Shore Lane | 5 S16 | Springdale Crescent | 32 B23 |
| Rosewell Place | 29 J16 | St Peter's Court | 8 T18 | Short Loanings | 4 P16 | Springdale Park | 32 C23 |
| Rosewell Terrace | 29 J16 | St Peters Gate (3) | 27 R13 | Sillerton Lane | 36 Q22 | Springdale Place | 32 C23 |
| Rosewood Avenue | 36 S23 | St Swithin Row | 6 M17 | Silverburn Crescent | 19 R7 | Springdale Road | 32 B23 |
| Roslin Place | 5 S15 | St Swithin Street | 6 M17 | Silverburn Place | 19 R7 | Springfield Avenue | 29 J18 |
| Roslin Street | 5 S14 | Salisbury Court | 35 N19 | Silverburn Road | 18 P8 | Springfield Gardens | 29 J19 |
| Roslin Terrace | 5 R15 | Salisbury Place | 35 N19 | Simpson Road | 19 R9 | Springfield Lane | 29 J18 |
| Ross Crescent | 25 J14 | Salisbury Terrace | 35 N19 | Sinclair Crescent | 39 T26 | Springfield Place | 29 J19 |
| Rousay Drive | 24 G15 | Salvesen Tower | 8 S17 | Sinclair Place | 39 T26 | Springfield Road | 28 H17 |
| Rousay Place | 24 G15 | Samprey Road | 28 F16 | Sinclair Road | 8 S18 | Springfield Road | 34 K20 |
| Rousay Terrace | 24 G15 | Sanday Road | 29 J16 | Sinclair Terrace | 39 T26 | Springhill Crescent | 24 G13 |
| Rowan Road | 26 L13 | Sandilands Drive | 26 N11 | Sir William Wallace | 19 R11 | Springhill Road | 24 G13 |
| Rowans, The | 33 F23 | Scalpay Walk (3) | 24 F15 | Wynd | | Springhill Terrace | 24 G13 |
| Royal Court | 29 L18 | School Avenue | 27 R12 | Skelly Rock | 39 T25 | (Northfield) | |
| Royfold Crescent | 29 K17 | School Drive | 27 R12 | Skene Lane | 4 P16 | Springhill Terrace (3) | 39 T27 |
| Rubislaw Cottages | 29 J18 | School Place | 27 S12 | Skene Place | 4 P16 | (Cove Bay) | |
| Rubislaw Den | 29 K17 | School Road (Cults) | 33 F23 | (Aberdeen) | | Stafford Street | 4 P14 |
| Gardens | | School Road (Seaton) | 27 R12 | Skene Place | 11 E3 | Stanley Street | 6 N17 |
| Rubislaw Den North | 29 L17 | School Terrace | 27 S12 | (Dyce) | | Station Mews (1) | 15 G9 |
| Rubislaw Den South | 29 L17 | School Walk | 27 S12 | Skene Road | 28 F16 | Station Road | 15 F8 |
| Rubislaw Park | 29 K18 | Schoolhill | 4 Q16 | Skene Square | 4 P15 | (Bankhead) | |
| Crescent | | Sclattie Circle | 15 E9 | Skene Street | 4 P16 | Station Road | 32 D24 |
| Rubislaw Park Road | 29 J18 | Sclattie Crescent | 15 E9 | Skene Terrace | 7 Q16 | (Bieldside) | |
| Rubislaw Place | 6 P17 | Sclattie Park | 15 E9 | Skye Road | 24 F15 | Station Road | 15 G9 |
| Rubislaw Terrace Lane | 6 N17 | Sclattie Place | 15 E10 | Slains Avenue | 18 P7 | (Bucksburn) | |
| Rubislaw Terrace | 6 N17 | Sclattie Walk | 15 E10 | Slains Circle | 12 N7 | Station Road (Cults) | 33 G22 |
| Ruby Lane | 7 Q16 | Scotstown Gardens | 19 R9 | Slains Lane | 12 P7 | Station Road (Dyce) | 11 E3 |
| Ruby Place | 7 Q16 | Scotstown Road | 13 Q7 | Slains Road | 12 N7 | Station Road | 17 M10 |
| Russell Road | 7 R18 | Scurdie Ness | 39 T25 | Slains Street | 12 N7 | (Woodside) | |
| Ruthrie Coast | 35 N20 | Scylla Drive | 39 S27 | Slains Terrace | 12 N7 | Stell Road | 7 R17 |
| Ruthrie Gardens | 35 M21 | Scylla Gardens | 39 S27 | Slessor Drive | 38 P24 | Stephen Place | 4 Q14 |
| Ruthrie Road | 35 M21 | Scylla Grove | 39 S27 | Slessor Road | 38 P24 | Stevenson Court | 4 P16 |
| Ruthrie Terrace | 35 M21 | Seafield Avenue | 29 K19 | Sluie Drive | 11 F2 | Stewart Crescent | 25 H12 |
| Ruthriehill Road | 15 F6 | Seafield Court | 29 K19 | Smithfield Road | 17 M11 | Stewart Park Court | 26 L12 |
| Ruthrieston Circle | 35 N20 | Seafield Crescent | 29 K19 | Smithfield Court | 25 K11 | Stewart Park Place | 26 L12 |
| Ruthrieston Court | 35 N20 | Seafield Drive East | 29 K18 | Smithfield Drive | 25 K11 | Stewart Terrace | 25 H12 |
| Ruthrieston Crescent | 35 N20 | Seafield Drive West | 29 K19 | Smithfield Lane | 17 L10 | Stirling Street | 7 R16 |
| Ruthrieston Gardens | 35 N21 | Seafield Gardens | 29 K19 | Smithyhaugh Road | 24 G11 | Stocket Parade | 25 K13 |
| Ruthrieston Place | 35 N20 | Seafield Road | 29 K19 | Society Court | 17 M11 | Stockethill Avenue | 25 K14 |
| Ruthrieston Road | 35 N21 | Seaforth Road | 5 R14 | Society Lane | 17 M11 | Stockethill Court | 25 K13 |
| Ruthrieston Terrace | 35 N21 | Sealcraig Gardens | 39 S25 | Souter Head Road | 39 S24 | Stockethill Crescent | 25 K14 |
| St Andrew Court | 4 Q15 | Seamount Court | 4 R15 | South Anderson Drive | 35 M19 | Stockethill Grange | 25 K14 |
| St Andrew Street | 4 Q15 | Seamount Place | 4 R15 | South Avenue | 33 F23 | Stockethill Lane (2) | 25 K14 |
| St Anne's Court | 4 Q14 | Seamount Road | 4 R15 | South College Street | 7 R17 | Stockethill Place | 25 K14 |
| St Catherine's Wynd | 5 R16 | Seaton Avenue | 27 R12 | South Constitution | 5 S15 | Stockethill Square | 25 K14 |
| St Clair Street | 5 R15 | Seaton Crescent | 27 S12 | Street | | Stockethill Way | 25 K13 |
| St Clement Street | 8 T16 | Seaton Drive | 27 R11 | South Crown Street | 7 Q18 | Stonehaven Road | 35 N23 |
| St Clement Place | 8 T16 | Seaton Gardens | 27 R11 | South Esplanade East | 8 S18 | Stoneyhill Terrace | 39 T27 |
| St Devenick's Place | 33 F23 | Seaton House | 27 S12 | South Esplanade West | 8 S18 | Stoneyton Terrace | 15 E8 |
| St Devenick's | 33 G23 | Seaton Place East | 27 R11 | South Grampian | 36 S19 | Stoneywood Park | 11 F5 |
| Crescent | | Seaton Place | 27 R11 | Circle | | North | |
| St Devenick's | 33 G23 | Seaton Road | 27 S12 | South Mount Street | 4 P15 | Stoneywood Park | 11 F5 |
| Terrace | | Seaton Walk | 27 R11 | South Silver Street | 7 Q16 | Stoneywood Road | 11 E5 |
| St Fittick's Road | 9 V18 | Seaview Avenue | 13 R4 | South Square | 9 U17 | Stoneywood Road | 15 F7 |
| St John's Place | 7 Q17 | Seaview Circle | 13 R5 | South Stocket | 25 K13 | Stoneywood Terrace | 15 F6 |
| St John's Road | 15 G9 | Seaview Close | 13 R4 | Lane (1) | | Stornoway Crescent | 24 E14 |

| | | | | | | | |
|---|---|---|---|---|---|---|---|
| Strachan Mill Court | 4 P16 | Todhead Gardens | 39 T25 | Wallacebrae Crescent | 17 L8 | Westholme Terrace | 29 J17 |
| Strachan Place | 25 K11 | Todlaw Walk | 11 F2 | Wallacebrae Drive | 17 L8 | Westray Crescent | 25 J15 |
| Strachan's Lane | 6 P18 | Tollohill Crescent | 36 R22 | Wallacebrae Gardens | 17 L8 | Westray Road | 25 H15 |
| Strathbeg Place (3) | 18 Q9 | Tollohill Drive | 36 R23 | Wallacebrae Path | 17 L8 | Westwood Place | 15 F10 |
| Strathburn Street | 39 S25 | Tollohill Gardens | 36 R22 | Wallacebrae Place | 17 K8 | Whin Park Place | 25 H13 |
| Strathmore Drive | 25 H13 | Tollohill Lane | 36 Q22 | Wallacebrae Road | 17 L8 | Whin Park Road | 25 H12 |
| Strawberry Bank Parade | 7 P17 | Tollohill Place | 36 R22 | Wallacebrae Terrace | 17 K8 | Whinhill Gardens | 35 Q19 |
| | | Tollohill Square | 36 Q23 | Wallacebrae Walk | 17 K8 | Whinhill Gate | 7 Q18 |
| Stroma Terrace | 24 F15 | Tornashean Gardens | 11 F2 | Wallacebrae Wynd | 17 L8 | Whinhill Road | 7 Q18 |
| Stronsay Avenue | 28 H16 | Trinity Lane | 7 R16 | Wallfield Crescent | 6 N16 | Whitehall Mews | 6 N16 |
| Stronsay Crescent | 28 H16 | Trinity Shopping Centre | 7 Q16 | Wallfield Place | 6 N16 | Whitehall Place | 6 N16 |
| Stronsay Drive | 28 H16 | | | Walton Road (Dyce) | 10 B3 | Whitehall Road | 6 M16 |
| Stronsay Place | 28 H16 | Trinity Street | 7 R16 | Walton Road (Greenburn) | 14 B6 | Whitehall Terrace | 6 N16 |
| Sugarhouse Lane | 5 S16 | Tulloch Park | 15 E10 | | | Whitehills Crescent | 39 S26 |
| Sumburgh Crescent | 24 F14 | Tullos Circle | 36 S19 | Wapping Street | 7 R17 | Whitehills Rise | 39 S27 |
| Summer Place | 11 E3 | Tullos Crescent | 36 T19 | Wardhead Place | 24 G14 | Whitehills Way | 39 S26 |
| Summer Street | 26 N11 | Tullos Place | 36 T19 | Watchman Brae | 24 E11 | Whitehouse Street | 7 P16 |
| Summer Street | 7 Q16 | Turnberry Court | 18 P7 | Water Lane | 5 S16 | Whitemyres Place | 25 J15 |
| Summerfield Place | 5 S15 | Turnberry Crescent | 18 Q7 | Waterloo Quay | 8 T16 | Whitemyres Avenue | 25 H15 |
| Summerfield Terrace | 5 R15 | Turnberry Gardens | 18 Q7 | Waterton Road | 15 F7 | Whitestripes Avenue | 12 M7 |
| Summerhill Court | 25 J15 | Two Mile Cross | 35 M22 | Watson Lane | 26 N15 | Whitestripes Close | 12 N7 |
| Summerhill Crescent | 25 J15 | Ugie Place | 25 H14 | Watson Street | 26 N15 | Whitestripes Crescent | 12 N7 |
| Summerhill Drive | 28 H16 | Uist Road | 24 F15 | Waulkmill Crescent | 25 H11 | Whitestripes Drive | 12 M6 |
| Summerhill Road | 29 J16 | Union Glen | 7 P17 | Waulkmill Road | 24 G12 | Whitestripes Path | 12 N7 |
| Summerhill Terrace | 29 J16 | Union Glen Court | 7 P17 | Wavell Crescent | 18 N10 | Whitestripes Place | 12 N7 |
| Sunert Road | 32 A25 | Union Grove Lane | 6 M18 | Wavell House | 18 Q10 | Whitestripes Road | 12 M7 |
| Sunny Brae | 15 E10 | Union Grove | 6 M18 | Waverley Lane | 6 P17 | Whitestripes Street | 12 N7 |
| Sunnybank Place | 27 Q13 | Union Grove Court | 6 P17 | Waverley Place | 6 P17 | Whitestripes Way | 12 N6 |
| Sunnybank Road | 27 Q13 | Union Row (Aberdeen) | 7 Q17 | Weavers Row | 25 H12 | Wilkie Avenue | 17 K11 |
| Sunnybrae Cottages | 17 K9 | Union Row (Dyce) | 11 E3 | Webster Road | 35 P23 | Willowbank Road | 7 P18 |
| Sunnyside Avenue | 27 Q13 | Union Street | 7 Q17 | Weigh House Square | 5 S16 | Willowdale Place | 4 R15 |
| Sunnyside Gardens | 27 Q13 | Union Terrace | 7 Q16 | Wellbrae Terrace | 29 L19 | Willowgate Close | 7 P17 |
| Sunnyside Road | 27 Q13 | Union Wynd | 7 Q16 | Wellheads Crescent | 11 E5 | Willowpark Crescent | 25 J14 |
| Sunnyside Terrace | 27 Q13 | University Road | 27 Q12 | Wellheads Drive | 11 E5 | Willowpark Place | 25 J14 |
| Sunnyside Walk | 27 Q13 | University Court | 15 E10 | Wellheads Road | 14 D6 | Willowpark Road | 25 J14 |
| Swannay Road | 24 G15 | Upper Denbush | 4 P16 | Wellheads Place | 11 E5 | Windford Road | 24 G15 |
| Swannay Square | 24 F15 | Upper Farburn Road | 10 C4 | Wellheads Road | 11 F4 | Windford Square | 24 G15 |
| Sycamore Place | 35 Q19 | Upper Mastrick Way | 25 H13 | Wellheads Terrace | 15 E6 | Windmill Brae | 7 Q17 |
| Talisman Drive | 34 K22 | Upperkirkgate | 4 R16 | Wellheads Way | 11 E5 | Windmill Lane | 7 Q17 |
| Talisman Road | 34 K22 | Urquhart Lane | 5 S14 | Wellington Brae (3) | 36 R19 | Windsor Place | 6 P17 |
| Talisman Walk | 34 K22 | Urquhart Place | 5 S14 | Wellington Circle | 38 R24 | Wingate Place | 18 P11 |
| Tanfield Avenue | 26 N11 | Urquhart Road | 5 R14 | Wellington Place | 7 R17 | Wingate Road | 18 P11 |
| Tanfield Court | 26 N11 | Urquhart Street | 5 S14 | Wellington Road | 38 P28 | Wood Street | 8 U18 |
| Tanfield Walk | 26 N11 | Urquhart Terrace | 5 S14 | Wellington Road | 36 R20 | Woodburn Avenue | 28 H18 |
| Taransay Court | 24 F14 | Usan Ness | 39 T25 | Wellington Street | 8 T16 | Woodburn Crescent | 28 H18 |
| Taransay Crescent | 24 F14 | Valentine Crescent | 18 N7 | Wellwood Cottages | 33 G22 | Woodburn Gardens | 28 H18 |
| Taransay Road | 24 F15 | Valentine Drive | 18 M8 | Wellwood Terrace | 33 G22 | Woodburn Place | 28 H18 |
| Tarbothill Road | 18 Q9 | Valentine Road | 12 M7 | West Cairncry Road | 25 K13 | Woodcroft Avenue | 12 M4 |
| Tay Road | 25 H13 | Valley Crescent | 36 R22 | West Craibstone Street | 7 Q17 | Woodcroft Gardens | 12 M4 |
| Tedder Road | 26 P11 | Valley Gardens | 36 Q22 | West Cults Road | 33 E24 | Woodcroft Grove | 12 M4 |
| Tedder Street | 26 P11 | Victoria House | 5 R15 | West Mount Street | 4 P15 | Woodcroft Road | 12 M4 |
| Tern Place | 13 R5 | Victoria Road | 8 T18 | West North Street | 5 R15 | Woodcroft Walk | 12 M4 |
| Tern Road | 39 S26 | Victoria Street (Aberdeen) | 6 P17 | West Tullos Road | 36 Q21 | Woodend Avenue | 28 G17 |
| Teviot Road | 24 G14 | | | Westburn Court | 4 P15 | Woodend Crescent | 28 G16 |
| Theatre Lane | 5 S16 | Victoria Street (Dyce) | 11 E3 | Westburn Drive | 26 M14 | Woodend Drive | 28 H16 |
| Thistle Court | 7 P16 | View Terrace | 4 P15 | Westburn Road | 25 K15 | Woodend Place | 28 H17 |
| Thistle Lane | 7 P17 | Viewfield Avenue | 29 K19 | Westburn Road | 26 N15 | Woodend Road | 28 H16 |
| Thistle Place | 7 P17 | Viewfield Court | 29 K19 | Western Road | 18 M11 | Woodend Terrace | 28 H16 |
| Thistle Road | 10 B4 | Viewfield Crescent | 29 K19 | Western Road | 26 N11 | Woodhill Court | 25 K14 |
| Thistle Street | 7 P17 | Viewfield Gardens | 29 J19 | Westerton | 25 H11 | Woodhill Place | 29 K16 |
| Thomas Glover Place | 18 Q9 | Viewfield Mews | 29 K18 | Crescent (7) | | Woodhill Road | 29 K16 |
| Thom's Court | 27 Q12 | Viewfield Road | 29 K19 | Westerton Crescent | 25 H12 | Woodhill Terrace | 29 K16 |
| Thom's Place | 27 Q12 | Virginia Street | 5 R16 | Westerton Place | 33 G23 | Woodlands Drive | 10 B3 |
| Thomson Street | 26 N15 | Wagley Court | 15 E10 | Westerton Place | 25 J11 | Woodlands Road | 10 B3 |
| Thorngrove Avenue | 29 L19 | Wagley Parade | 15 E10 | Westerton Road | 33 G22 | Woodside Road | 13 R6 |
| Thorngrove Court | 29 L19 | Wagley Place | 15 E10 | Westfield Road | 6 N16 | Woodstock Court | 29 L16 |
| Thorngrove Crescent | 29 L19 | Wagril's Lane (6) | 27 Q12 | Westfield Terrace | 6 N16 | Woodstock Road | 29 K16 |
| Thorngrove Place | 29 L19 | Wales Street | 5 S15 | Westgate | 15 E10 | Woolmanhill | 4 Q16 |
| Tillydrone Avenue | 27 Q11 | Walker Lane | 8 S18 | Westholme Avenue | 29 J17 | Wright's Coopers Place (5) | 27 Q12 |
| Tillydrone Court | 18 P10 | Walker Place | 36 S19 | Westholme Crescent North | 29 J17 | | |
| Tillydrone Road | 18 P10 | Walker Road | 8 S18 | | | York Place | 8 T16 |
| Tillydrone Terrace | 18 P11 | Wallace House | 28 G17 | Westholme Crescent South | 28 H17 | York Street | 8 T16 |
| Tiree Crescent | 24 F15 | Wallacebrae Avenue | 17 K8 | | | Ythan Road | 24 G14 |